SEA STORIES
Galveston & Beyond

Alvin L. Sallee
with Michael J. Leahy Jr.

To Adm. Mike —
Thanks for your service
to Seafarers & for the
story (page 67) for the
Fair Winds —
[signature] 2021

SEA STORIES
Copyright © 2021 by Alvin L. Sallee

ABQ Publishing
Printed in the United States of America
ISBN: 978-0-9991486-2-4

Praise for Galveston Wharf Stories
by Alvin L. Sallee

"In Galveston Wharf Stories: Captains, Characters & Cruises (2019), Sallee reveals the labyrinthine maze of politics, engineering, and economics of a thriving wharf. Whether a maritime professional who makes a living from the sea or someone interested in the salty life, Sallee's books more than whet the appetite." Donna Gable Hatch, Galveston Monthly.com

"Many a sailor tells their stories in dimly lit bars. Not Alvin Sallee. You can smell the brisk salt air, feel the wind in your face, and the hear the seagulls overhead. His book, Galveston Wharf Stories, teems with humor and history, not only of Galveston but of the people of the wharf and beyond, the sentinels of the port." Dr. William V. Flores, co-author Democracy, Civic Engagement and Citizenship in Higher Education.

"Alvin Sallee's Galveston Wharf Stories: Captains, Characters & Cruises is a winner for many reasons, but the one that tops my list is that it tells the truth. And it's written in a very charming way." Bill Cherry, author Bill Cherry's Galveston Memories

"Personal anecdotes and experiences of the author written in a concise, conversational manner engaged me on a journey of discovery. The journey to other ports opened doors to me to other worlds I have not experienced, broadening my understanding of other cultures and lifestyles. Personalities and character sketches of people met along the way made this historical travelogue an interesting book to read." Phyllis Townsend

"Galveston Wharf Stories is a great collection of behind the scenes activity on the wharf. I was especially fascinated by all the historic references that go well beyond Galveston and tying in many parts of the Caribbean. Not only entertaining but a great reference book as well." Fritz Damler, author Ten Years Behind the Mast: The Voyage of Theodora R.

Table of Contents

Introduction

At first glance, Alvin Sallee and Mike Leahy might seem unlikely collaborators for a collection of stories about life on and near the sea. But while they have vastly different backgrounds— Sallee was a professor of social work spanning decades, Leahy an engineer on massive ocean-going ships—they share a quality essential for good storytelling: curiosity. About the world. About the sea. About how things work. And about people, always people.

For years, *Galveston Daily News* readers enjoyed Sallee's columns showcasing the personalities, legends, and lore of that city's famous wharves and beyond. His first book, *Galveston Wharf Stories*, collected those columns so fans old and new could access them in one place.

Soon, with further time on ships, wharves and on journeys, Sallee had more to share, more to say, and began assembling *Sea Stories*.

Enter Mike Leahy.

First as a reader of Sallee's column (see next page: *How This Venture Began*), and then as a friend and trader of tales both water and land-bound, Sallee quickly realized that Mike Leahy told stories that few others could. His intimate knowledge of the innermost workings of big ships, paired with remarkable experiences while at sea and ashore in ports around the globe, make for reading that's both engaging and informative. (For a guide to any unfamiliar maritime terms, check out the glossary at the back of the book.)

From Sallee's signature profiles of people whose lives have been shaped by the sea both in Galveston and worldwide, to Leahy's sometimes grueling, sometimes jaw-dropping escapades in faraway ports, *Sea Stories* readers will appreciate hearing two very different voices that celebrate the forever fascinating, forever alluring subject: *the sea.*

Mari Anderson
Co-Author, Plunge: Midlife with Snorkel
April, 2021

i

How this Venture Began

Sallee

Faux palm fronds hung over our heads, a cheap tropical vibe, for sure.

"What are you having?" he asked.

"Probably the Hula Burger—fat, juicy, with grilled pineapple."

"Hmm," came the response.

Two old guys. One a seafarer: Mike Leahy. The other a professor and writer: Alvin Sallee (that would be me).

Mike in a blue boiler suit with old oil stains, comfortable in his own skin. Me in a Hawaiian shirt, shorts and a straw Panama hat with a black band. Pen in hand, scribbling as fast as I could.

Both of us had landed in Galveston, one on 48th and Ave. Q, the other 46th and Ave. R. Close by, yet from lives far apart.

I was high-desert bred: Nuevo Mexico. First two years with Mom, following Dad from one naval yard to the next, Key West to Portsmouth.

Mike from Bayonne, New Jersey, born by the wharves while Dad was at sea.

The waitress, a young Texas A&M-Galveston student, rarely interrupted as questions and stories flew across the rough wooden table at the Hula Hut, just steps from the wharves of Galveston.

After interviewing Mike for a newspaper column that day, I continued to reach out to him for advice and information. Sometimes Susan, his wife, would join us for lunch, answering even more of my questions. These sessions were always over too quickly for me.

One day while Mike was paying the bill, I told Susan what a joy it was to chat with him. She looked at me, deadpan, and said, "Why do you think I married him?"

Over the years of publishing Galveston Wharf Stories columns in *The Galveston Daily News*, I received many insightful responses from Mike. Clearly, he knew the wharves, the local politics, and a bunch about ships, sometimes suggesting new avenues to explore. As I was preparing to write *Sea Stories*, it seemed only natural to invite Mike to contribute. I know that you, the reader, will be greatly informed and entertained by his real-life stories.

About the Authors

The Professor: Alvin L. Sallee, LISW, ACSW, Professor Emeritus, taught Social Work for 39 years. Thirty-three were at New Mexico State University (NMSU—the "other" Aggies) in the School of Social Work, serving 18 years as academic head. For another 15 years, he directed the NMSU Family Preservation Institute.

He has extensive national board and committee experience, authored nine books and over 50 articles and reports. He obtained over 50 grants and contracts totaling more than $15M ($30M in today's dollars). Over 30 universities including Turkey, Belize, Mexico and the U.S. employed Professor Sallee as a consultant.

For four years, he was a visiting professor at the University of Houston-Downtown, serving as Director of the Center for Family Strengths, a job which brought him to Galveston to live. Sallee still serves as an expert witness in child abuse cases.

He served as the volunteer president/CEO of the Cavalla Historical Foundation which operates the Galveston Naval Museum at Seawolf Park.

Retired, he wrote a weekly column for the *Galveston Daily News*, Texas's oldest newspaper, on the subject of the wharves and the folks who work them. When compiled, the columns morphed into the 2019 book, *Galveston Wharf Stories: Characters, Captains and Cruises*. Mike Leahy was one of the characters. Captain Vandy was both captain and character. Over 100 days at sea were the cruises.

In the summer of 2020, Alvin returned home to the mountains of New Mexico to help with his family. Each morning he reads *The Galveston Daily News* and looks way southeast toward the sea.

The Seafarer: Michael J. Leahy, Jr. is a third-generation marine engineer and seafarer. He spent 24 years going to sea, primarily onboard American steam tankers and freighters.

Passing on the opportunity to attend the U.S. Merchant Marine Academy, he chose instead to go to sea in unlicensed positions from ordinary seaman up to chief pumpman. He then joined the officer ranks after sitting for an original, unlimited, 3rd engineer's license, thus following the same path as his father and uncles.

He later raised his licenses and sailed as 2nd and 1st engineer. In 1995, wishing to have more regular time with his family, he opted to come ashore permanently as port engineer for sealift support ships of the U.S. Maritime Administration rather than take a chief engineer's job offered on a ship in the Far East.

He spent a further 25 years in shoreside management of commercial and U.S. government ships, as well as serving as vice president and general manager of a shipyard. He is presently an independent consultant engineer and marine surveyor.

Over the course of his career he has resided in the port cities of New York, Galveston, Mobile, San Francisco, Charleston, and New Orleans.

Acknowledgments

Our thanks to all the folks who shared their personal narratives, which conveyed a human face to every sea story. Thank you for your time and trust. You are each acknowledged in the following chapters. Thank you to the *Galveston County Daily News*, *Galveston Monthly Magazine's* John Hall, publisher, Kimber Fountain, editor, and Donna Gable Hatch, Bill Cherry, Rudy and Rich Biro, and John Zellmer for permission to share their work.

To the Cavalla Historical Foundation, Edsall Class Veterans Association, and crew at the Galveston Naval Museum, led by Chiefs Mac Christy, Ross Garcia and Aric Deuel, for maintaining these proud vessels and for their contributions to Chapters 7 and 8. Our sincere thanks to Cindy Dales for her father's, Arthur G. Rand, Jr. (USN), photos.

And for honest feedback and support, thanks to the ABQ writers group, George, Susan, Charles and Roz. Gratitude for our beta readers: Master Chief Ross Garcia, Merry Bell, Bonnie Rettig, Kelly McCully and Steven Sallee, careful review.

Thanks to the production team, without whom you would not have this book to read. Our gratitude for John Moore, eagle-eyed proofreader, Bill Cherry for making sure there is always a moral to the story, Heber Taylor for editing and publishing many wharf story columns, which opened many doors. Also to Mari Anderson, for putting it all together in a readable, presentable manner, Fritz Damler, for the ten years behind the mast, setting the course for telling tales, Susan Leahy for support and transforming photographs, Joan Sallee for bringing 1940s photos to the next century and Kathy Sallee for grammar reform and sustaining Alvin's writing addiction.

CHAPTER 1
Galveston: A Unique History

Carnival Triumph, now the Sunrise, rotates in narrow
Galveston Harbor before heading out to sea.

In this Chapter
Sallee

Galveston is distinctive, even for a seaport city. When we began writing this book both of us lived here, Mike for the fifth time, me, for the first time after years of visits. Now both of us have left, mostly for family reasons.

We hate to admit it, but this makes us typical. Seems many Islanders by Choice (IBC's) live here about 10 years and then move on. Born on the Islanders (BOI's) may leave, yet most return.

This chapter presents Galveston in all of its forms. The original port of Texas, Galveston has welcomed travelers from all over the world, especially eastern Europe for over 180 years. In fact, the

Galveston Immigration Station was second only to New York's Ellis Island in welcoming folks, many Jewish. Other groups came from Italy, Serbia, and Germany.

Kimber Fountain's *Tribute to Galveston* perfectly presents the past 180-year highlights, people, storms, along with the spirit that drives the resiliency of residents of this spit of sand. As Bill Cherry so aptly points out in his book, *Galveston Memories*, this is not a place for industry, but for people to enjoy living and visiting. And for meeting or being characters, as there are plenty in this town, past and present. Even dolphins and sharks—blacktips and hammerheads—are characters who love the waters of Galveston.

The storms and the resulting seawall are detailed in Galveston's Seawall Chronicles, and how hurricanes change the island. Real characters who made Galveston unique are presented through book reviews of the Maceo family, ladies of the night, George Mitchell, the savior of the Strand; and the hermit who lived on a sunken ship.

Enjoy your visit to Galveston before we begin our sea voyage to other wharves on cargo and cruise ships. And just in case you encounter an unfamiliar phrase or word along the way, please note we've included a glossary of maritime terms at the back of the book.

And now, it's time to cast off!

Sunrise on a Galveston morning. Note the first row of ships off shore waiting for their turn to come to port.

Galveston, an Island Port
Sallee

Heading for the wharf by way of Seawall Blvd. in this almost-light early spring morning, I see the soft backlit cloud bank in the distance. Fuchsia forms the bottom layer across the horizon laid on blue water, while white wavelets lick the wide beach.

This is an island.

Then ship silhouettes appear. More ships emerge as small shadows below the still murky opaque sky. Ships, lit, all the way to the horizon and over the edge of the Earth waiting to come to the wharves.

This is an anchorage city.

Parking in our special spot at the foot of Kuhn's Wharf, the sailor's song rings in my ear. *"Away ho, away ho!"* The dogs and I head toward the dock. Another early morning on the Galveston quay.

This is a sea shanty town.

Blonde light stretches up, then orange. A golden globe floats from the spectrum of color. The sun, like a Chinese lantern, shines a beam of light across the aquatic scene. (And they say I'm color

3

blind.) From Pier 21, I gaze down the harbor toward the sea as if on the bow of a ship.

This is a seaport.

Drawn to the dawn, the dogs and I trek east on the old wooden pier through the mosquito fleet of fishing boats, so named for their skinny masts. Twelve-year-old golden, Chloe, has a bounce in her stride. Smokey, a low to the ground dashador, motors along. At the end of the dock we turn from the dim rays to head west, toward the barely visible lines of the masts and yards of *Elissa*.

This is a sailing ship town.

We stroll under the iconic statue, *High Tide*. The green shades of bronze depict a shirtless, hair-blown, smiling boy in dungarees perched way atop a wharf piling, hand stretched out to feed the gulls. (A practice frowned upon by Islanders.)

Charles Parks' 1992 sculpture greets the sun each morn, and tourists all day, here on the wharf. Galveston is a tourist town; we are all drawn down to the sea.

High Tide statue on Pier 21.

4

Nearby, still asleep on a bench, is a gentleman straight out of casting from *Pirates of the Caribbean*. Bushy sideburns, a ponytail of grey, a bike with efficiently loaded baskets and bag tied to the end—all of his possessions.

This is a seaport.

Regrettably, I turn my back to the water and return to the Kuhn Wharf sign. Harborside Blvd. has turned into the Indy 500 Speedway as insurance and medical employees from off the Island race to work on the East End.

This is a seafarer hospital town.

The sun is higher, the city alive. Another day in an affordable paradise, even for people who live on the street. This morning, at 0600 hours, a group of about eight folks, without homes, gather as usual near the golden arches, sipping hot coffee.

This is a haven town.

Just yesterday Capt. Gary Bell commented, "Galveston is such a unique place." He should know. A retired submarine captain, he has seen the world, even if he was under the sea for over two full years. Now as chair of the Cavalla Historical Foundation, which operates the Galveston Naval Museum in Seawolf Park, he is still on the sea.

This is an historic town.

We walk down 23rd Street toward the wharves, past Coffee Roaster's, Tammy at the insurance office, Bill Cherry's former Star Drugstore. I yell "Hi" to Cruz, the Hawaiian shirt store guy. I have a brief conversation about the day with a stranger who becomes an instant friend.

Galveston is a seaport to the world kind of town.

Unique, and filled with stories, here and beyond.

Galveston Seaport Chaplain
Sallee

"When I started doing chaplain work aboard ships, crew members always wanted to talk to the male chaplain. They would ask me what are you doing here? That was 35 years ago. But, I still am afraid to climb gangways," Karen Parsons confided.

We had just climbed a very long gangway up the side of an empty bulk cargo ship tied to Pier 39 in Galveston. This gangway was set on angle so we actually were walking on the edge of each step, not the regular flat part. I had taken two steps at a time with my long legs and yes, I had trouble keeping up with her. On the way down, she was on the ground before I was halfway.

As we walked towards the Seafarers Center van, I commented, "Well, you certainly went down that gangway fast. You must not be afraid of them anymore. "

She laughed, "Oh, I am afraid, I want to get it over fast."

Not many women, even strong women, are brave enough to board foreign cargo ships full of unknown men to spread the word and explain what is available at the seafarers center.

Today when Karen Parsons comes aboard the men smile. They know why she is there even though they may have never met her.

Seafarers centers are found all around the world and ship crews have a very effective network to share information on each port. Most Seafarers' Centers provide a home away from home and more importantly, Internet service.

The key to unlocking the crew members is to ask them about their family. Karen begins by asking, "Are you married?" If the answer is yes, the next question is, "Do you have children?"

So far, the answer has always been "yes" when I have heard the question. Next, "How old are the children?" and then the men are off and running telling their life stories, their plans, and how much they miss their family. Not only is there an emphasis on family in the United States, there is a real focus on families all over the world.

Karen also asks about their present home, the ship. Crewmembers share a detailed history, where it was built, what country each crew came from and where they spend their time. In this case, they say it was launched four years ago and both Karen and I are surprised that it was that new.

She asked how long has there has been a Filipino crew onboard. The first year the ship was crewed and operated by the Chinese. As we leave Karen said, "Clearly the first crew was very hard on the vessel."

Rarely do we catch most of the crew at one time, even in port as the crew stands watch, or sleeps. And yet, if there were crew around, after 55 days at sea, they probably have heard each other's stories over and over.

For part of the 1.6 million seafarers, Chaplain Karen is a welcome respite in their routine. To volunteer contact: *www.galvestonseafarerscenter.org*

End Note:

Chaplain Karen Parsons retired her post as the archdiocesan port chaplain for the ports of Galveston and Texas City on Dec. 30, 2020. For 28 years, from her base at the Galveston Seafarers Center, 221 20th St. she challenged both her fear of heights and water to provide care to the men and women who came on ships into the Port of Galveston, regardless of race, religion, nationality or political beliefs.

*Modern day Ro/Ro ship, Michigan Highway, passes
1877 sail ship Elissa in Galveston Harbor.*

The Spirit of the Island
By Kimber Fountain in Galveston Monthly Magazine, September 2019 (used with permission)

At the bleakest moment in Galveston's history, when the stench of death was covered only by the smoke of funeral pyres, when a 20-foot-high, 8-mile-long debris wall—all that remained of the southern half of the island—loomed over downtown, at a time when the joy of reuniting with a loved one was cruelly tempered by the loss of a dozen others, news outlets around the country were quick to proclaim that "Galveston was finished." No city could survive the magnitude of the destruction left behind by that September storm.

They had forgotten that Galveston was not a city of mere mortals, it was a city of dreamers, renegades, trailblazers, and die-hards. The naysayers neglected to realize that everything that had transpired upon the shores of the island city since its 1839 inception was not mere luck nor chance, but rather, an outpouring of an unexplainable, intangible force of unyielding determination, a magnetism forged by a collective genius, creativity, and ambition.

The rapid and vast commercial successes borne from this incubator in the 19th Century were looked upon by outsiders with both awe and contempt, especially as the bravado manifested itself by way of a mansion-building contest along Broadway Avenue and a downtown replete with architectural masterpieces. However, what were seen by some as ostentatious displays of wealth were in fact a people giving back to their benefactor, installations of jewels upon the crown of the Queen City of the Gulf.

But only now, as Galveston suffered in agony at the hands of her nemesis Mother Nature, was the unseen force behind the city's meteoric rise given a name. Surrounded by rubble and ruin, facing a population stricken by the pain of the recent past and fear for the future, Isaac H. "Ike" Kempner declared that "The Spirit of Galveston" would prevail.

This spirit had given the island its paradisiacal status, not the water or the weather, just as it had catapulted Galveston from a modest trading post to a thriving port of international commerce. It was the spirit that would lift the city from tragedy to affluence as it had once before, and as it would again and again.

Galveston was still an infant city the first time that uncontrollable circumstances overshadowed its natural proclivity for prosperity. When the nation fractured in 1861, a federal blockade was launched against all southern seaports, crippling Galveston's burgeoning economy. A handful of daring businessmen maneuvered the Civil War situation with blockade runners, but the remainder of the population evacuated their island home as it became consumed with military activity.

As the closest port city to Mexico, a Union ally, Galveston was viewed as a strategic piece of the supply chain. In late 1862, northern forces wrestled control from their southern counterparts, but with a surprise attack during the early morning hours of New Year's Day 1863, known historically as the Battle of Galveston, the Confederacy regained control and maintained it for the duration of the war.

During Restoration, Galveston patiently endured the interference of the federal government and subsequently managed to outpace almost every other southern city with its rapid rebound. This feverish quest for economic dominance continued unfettered for the rest of the 19th century, elevating Galveston's commerce to a level that surpassed even that of New Orleans.

The population was the second wealthiest (per capita) in the nation, just beneath that of Newport, Rhode Island, home of the Vanderbilt dynasty. Equally as important to the city's fabric was its port of immigration that once surpassed Ellis Island.

This widespread and multi-faceted international influence enlivened the city census to reflect an eclectic mix of nationalities and infused the town with diversity. Among the open-minded population, who lived in unrestricted and unsegregated residential areas, a person's only meaningful designation was that of "Islander."

Indeed, only a population galvanized by this social and economic success, as well as the pride elicited by such an accomplishment, was strong enough to embrace the overwhelming task of recovering from the 1900 Storm. Interestingly, most historians deny Galveston this, its grandest achievement, and instead the storm is often named as the ultimate abdication of its sovereignty. But the city did not merely rebuild structures, it literally raised itself to new heights.

Determined to never let future generations of islanders endure such a hardship and emboldened by The Spirit of Galveston, the city on a sandbar enacted what is still today considered one of the most significant feats of civil engineering ever accomplished in the history of the United States. They built a 17-foot-high barricade against the sea and elevated the southern half of the island an average of 13 feet; the original seawall and ensuing grade-raising took nearly a decade to complete.

Meanwhile on the northern shore, the Port of Galveston was endowed with the most technologically advanced wharf in the world where it continued to shatter records of importation and exportation set prior to the storm.

When at last its commerce was overtaken in 1914 with the opening of the Houston Ship Channel, Galveston yet again refused to cower amid adversity. The sense of invincibility fostered by its early success and superlative recovery created the ideal conditions for the city to unofficially declare itself "The Free State of Galveston."

Continuing as it had previously, undaunted by outside opinion, the city chose to again play by its own rules - even if that meant changing the game. The eventual and ugly demise of the Free State has relegated this era of Galveston history to the bottom of the heap, but that does not erase the fact that this era is perhaps the most potent example of The Spirit of Galveston.

The winners write history, which is why few people know about a certain coastal community's ability to transform the non-violent, victimless "crimes" of vice into a famed national reputation for glamour, luxury, and elegance that removed Galveston from of the atrocities of war and depression. These same sins, for which the city paid dearly in 1957 with a violent and nationally embarrassing takedown at the hands of self-serving state officials, are the ones that today have made Las Vegas an international sensation.

It seemed at the time that The Spirit of Galveston had been rendered extinct, both sunken and set ablaze like the confiscated slot machines that were once as ubiquitous as the mindset that had installed them in every drugstore and washateria in town. Then Hurricane Carla (1961) grabbed the city by the shoulders and shook it admonishingly, reminding Galveston that the spirit could be buried, but it would never die. Although they no longer exist, the prominent accomplishments of the decade after Carla, namely the Flagship Hotel and Sea-Arama, marked the island's entrance into a new era that has yet to be named but continues to evolve.

Weakened from a century of hardship, Galveston finally seemed willing to succumb to the opinion imposed onto it from the outside - that it had always and would always be worthy only of beach-town status, laden with family-friendly entertainment for the rest of the world to enjoy, even if it was not a true embodiment of the city's values. Thus, although the spirit had been renewed, it limped along with apathy at the task set before it.

At last in the 1980s, a hometown boy turned oil magnate lit the spark that continues to burn. Perhaps the singular definer of the modern spirit, George Mitchell started the conversation that was finally brought to the forefront after Hurricane Ike again tested the city's strength—Galveston is more, so much more, than a beach town.

Just ask one of the hundreds of artists, small business owners, or non-profit organizations who have breathed life into Galveston's historic downtown, or one of the thousands of historic homeowners who have personally invested in immortalizing island history. They will tell you that the vibrant and exponential growth over the last ten years has nothing to do with a coat of paint, a new building, or a repaved sidewalk.

They will tell you, or rather show you, that the Spirit of Galveston is alive and well.

*Galveston's 1900 storm memorial on the seawall. Morning's
barely visible rain with soft grey clouds set the somber mood.*

Remembering the Great Storm
Sallee

Just across Seawall Blvd. from the San Luis Hotel is one of
Galveston's famous statues, a reminder of the power of nature. It
sits in a concrete park on the seawall on the edge of the beach with
its back to the sea.

"With one hand stretched out to the sky and other wrapped
around a woman and child, the figure depicted in Galveston's
1900 Storm Memorial", as John Wayne Ferguson, wrote in the
Galveston Daily News on September 8, 2015, makes a desperate
grasp for air before being taken by the sea.

Written 115 years after the hurricane which killed between
8,000 and 10,000 souls, he points out that Galveston still stands.
The David W. Moore statue was originally intended for Sea Wolf
Park in the 1980's. More than ten years later the Commission for
the Arts asked him to finish the work. It was placed at 48th and
Seawall where it stands today, often photographed.

This is one of my favorite Galveston spots—the dogs probably wonder why we stop here so often and just stare out at the sea.

Chloe staring out at the Gulf from on the seawall.

The Galveston Seawall
Review by Donna Gable Hatch, Galveston Monthly Magazine (used with permission)

Renowned Texas historian and author Melanie Wiggins said the *Galveston Seawall Chronicles*, a new book by Kimber Fountain, is an important untold chapter in the documented history of Galveston Island.

The seawall, considered by many to be the most impressive engineering feat in the history of the United States, has been included in historical publications, but never has it been the focus of an entire book until now, Wiggins said.

A City United
The seawall's story began on September 8, 1900, when the deadliest, most destructive hurricane in U.S. history on record to date, roared onto Galveston Island. The Category 4 hurricane made landfall with recorded winds of up to 156 mph and a storm surge that reached a height of 15 feet above the island's sandy grade. The catastrophic storm caused anywhere from 8,000 to

12,000 deaths and approximately $700 million in property damage in today's currency.

City leaders formed a three-member Board of Engineers—Alfred Noble, one of the best known civil engineers in the country; Henry Martyn Robert, a former chief engineer with the U.S. Army Corps of Engineers; and Henry Clay Ripley, a civil engineer with the Army Corps of Engineers in Galveston—and tasked the engineers to find a way to protect the city against Mother Nature's fury.

The committee recommended construction of a seawall 17 feet above mean low tide and stretching over three miles, from the south jetty across the eastern edge of the city and down the beach. The project also would require a Herculean engineering feat: More than 2,100 buildings, streetcar tracks, water pipes and fire hydrants—500 city blocks, some structures by a few inches and others by as much as 11 feet—had to be raised on hand-turned jackscrews, ratcheted up 1/4 inch at a time.

Galveston Seawall in1905, a year after its construction. Photo courtesy Kimber Fountain, Galveston Monthly Magazine.

"The grade-raising was a colossal undertaking; enormous dredges had to be brought in to pump sand from offshore into the areas behind the seawall, and people had to walk on wooden planks to cross streets," said Wiggins, a member of the Galveston County Historical Commission.

The cost of construction of the seawall and raising the city's infrastructure was an astronomical $6 million—$140 million in today's currency. Galveston County agreed to partially fund the cost for the seawall through a bond issue. The cost of raising each structure, however, was left to the owner of the building, and nearly every owner found the funds to do so. Not one dime of the project was federally funded.

In the decades that followed, the three-mile long seawall was extended five more times. Today, it is more than 10 miles long, stretching across one-third of Galveston's Gulf of Mexico frontage.

Galveston's Red Light District
Review by Donna Gable Hatch, Galveston Monthly Magazine (used with permission)

The history of Galveston is as interesting as it comes: pirates, gangland criminals, historic weather events, gorgeous architecture, money, money, money, and corruption.

In *Galveston's Red Light District: A History of the Line*, author Kimber Fountain shines a light on the underbelly of Galveston and its red light district, an area of very busy brothels encompassing a disproportionate area of the city. It was known by those who worked there and by their customers as The Line.

Her book scrapes off the barnacles of time and examines the torrid but tolerated symbiotic relationship between all those who profited from The Line's success in an era of Victorian morality. The focus is not restricted to the madams and prostitutes but also on the pillars of the community who not only turned a blind eye to the illicit trade but also profited from it and were all too happy to themselves partake of what it offered.

The old city of Galveston seemed to spread its wings protectively around its harbor, with its back to the sea offering safety and comfort to visiting ships and the seafarers manning them. The harbor lines the bank of a channel shaped like a crescent moon, but it is not this line to which Fountain's book pertains.

From its earliest days, mariners, including the infamous pirate Jean Lafitte, recognized the value of the deep-water harbor and used it as a safe haven for his ships and crews and as a base of operations for his illicit adventures.

The nation's navy eventually booted him off the island, but the spirit of Lafitte—including his penchant for illicit pursuits—was harder to jettison. That independent spirit and disregard for the finer points of law brought the city wealth, as well as national prominence and a rather complicated reputation as Sin City of the South.

In her book, Fountain relates the city's past as a beehive of activity. Sailors, soldiers, gamblers, and adventurers with pockets full of cash were welcomed with open arms by madams with stables of willing girls, gambling halls and saloon owners who flaunted prohibition with abandon.

The city had an uncanny ability to morph and accommodate what its residents and visitors wanted—and for a time, it wanted to indulge an almost insatiable appetite for lust. It became the playground for movie stars, luminaries, assorted bigwigs and crime bosses who came to enjoy a brand of good times unavailable anywhere else in the country.

Fountain's love of the tale and of the island itself intertwine as she points to the closets where the skeletons are hiding and connects them to the past with a visceral grip.

She introduces us to clever and savvy madams who amassed fortunes conducting business in the parlors of their "rooming houses" and provides insight into the lives of their hard-working stables of girls.

She describes the deals that were sealed with a nod and a handshake in the back rooms of City Hall or perhaps in the cozier settings of a particular madam's private boudoir.

The author delivers a bare-knuckle, impossible to resist tale about Galveston's seedy past and the social, financial, and political forces that provided the fuel that kept the Line humming and the public's fascination with Galveston on the front burner.

Galveston's Red Light District: A History of The Line, by Kimber Fountain, 2018, Arcadia Publishing-The History Press

The Free State of Galveston
Review by Donna Gable Hatch Galveston Monthly Magazine (used with permission)

Kimber Fountain's book, *The Maceos and the Free State of Galveston*, an authorized biography of the Maceo family and its ties to the history of the island—goes far beyond the underground gambling establishments and bootlegging and into the family's philanthropic and cultural legacy.

The 187-page book, which examines the family's legacy in chronological fashion, includes interviews with prominent members of the oh-so-fascinating family: Ronald Maceo, owner of Maceo Spice & Imports—and the grandson of Frank Maceo, who was cousin to Salvatore "Sam" and Rosario "Rose" Maceo, patriarchs of the Maceo empire; his children, Concetta Maceo-Sims and Frank Maceo; Vic Maceo, son of Sam and Rose's nephew Vic A. "Gigolo" Maceo; Marlina Maceo, granddaughter of Dutch Voight, the former leader of the Beach Gang who married Estelle Maceo; and a longtime family friend Saralyn Richardson, a fellow Galveston author.

While conducting research, Fountain pored through historic archives and photos—some that have never before been published, as well as photos of an anonymous collector's vast collection of Maceo memorabilia and ephemera from their clubs—to capture the essence of the Maceos and the family's landmark businesses.

Maceo Spice & Imports is renowned to foodies for its muffulettas, similar to an Italian sub and amazingly delicious, which can be traced back to R.S. Maceo (father of Ronald) who made and sold the now quintessential New Orleans sandwich from a wooden wagon in the city's French Quarter. But the family's influence on Galveston consists of much more than *cuisine gastronomique* and *herbes et epices*.

"The Maceos singlehandedly made art and culture important in Galveston," Fountain explains. "They were the sole creative impetus behind the establishment of Galveston as a purveyor of fine art and entertainment. Today, that is such a key piece of our city's identity and culture that it is hard to imagine Galveston without it."

She continues, "Prior to the Maceos, we were primarily a commercial center: Galveston's whole 'world' really centered on the international port. But then the Houston Ship Channel opened in 1914, and Galveston was forced to reevaluate its economic structure. This was helped along by the seawall—even though it had been built merely as a protective measure, which had slowly become the foundation for a new economy centered on entertainment. In turn, this provided the perfect conditions for the Maceos, who were born entertainers and visionaries, to use this newfound realization to catapult Galveston into an era of prosperity."

The Maceos and The Free State of Galveston, Kimber Fountain, 2020, The History Press
Online at www.arcadiapublishing.com
In stores at booksellers throughout Galveston and Houston
ebook at www.amazon.com

Savior of the Strand
Review by Alvin L. Sallee

If a first-generation immigrant saved his hometown, turning it into a national historic destination, you would probably know about him. Still, few know the real George P. Mitchell—until now.

Loren C. Steffy, a former Houston Chronicle financial reporter, has revealed a complex, still uncomplicated, Greek emigrants' son who through his dogged determination created change that benefits all Americans. His life is a tale of all the best opportunities the United States can offer a boy born into poverty near the wharves of Galveston.

George's father, Savvas Paraskevopoulos, a newly arrived teenager from Greece in the 1890s, had to change his name to Mike Mitchell when he worked for the railroad to be paid. Even with the name change, Savvas "was still a young man in a strange land, far from home and family." "His command of English remained rudimentary for years."

Steffy details the influence the Mitchell family had on George: a strong, fun mother, and three boys and a girl, each with their own personality. Christie, the Beachcomber, with calm Maria and outgoing Johnny, George's older brother. Later, Johnny was George's business partner. They would catch fish, selling them to tourists for $2, thus providing husbands an alibi when they visited Galveston.

This ability to leverage served George well throughout his business career. Johnny did not fare so well in his attempts as an oilman. Sam Maceo became Johnny's partner. After George graduated with his geology degree, thanks to money from the Maceos, and thanks to George's uncanny ability to spot oil in the ground, the partnership took off. Success included Lafitte's gold—oil—under Galveston.

Under Steffy's pen, the business and family sides of George Mitchell's life reads like a novel. The boom and bust in oil; developing the Woodlands, planned as a cure to urban blight; 10 kids with Cynthia, a career wanting wife; plus, the restoration of his home town are carefully documented. Details—George Mitchell was a reserved, highly inquisitive man who played tennis every day—are shared with journalistic care; the good and bad are objectively presented.

And myths are pushed back. Mitchell did not invent a tool to frack oil. Nonetheless, without 17 years of determination to develop his slick water recipe, fracking would never have worked. The U.S. would still be importing oil at much higher prices. Fracking problems were caused later by greedy companies, not by the environmentalist George Mitchell.

The Woodlands was personally designed by Mitchell so people of all colors, from janitors to the wealthy, could live next to each other. But new owners created just another wealthy Houston suburb.

With his wealth, Mitchell returned to his home town and rebuilt the Strand—the downtown of Galveston, which had fallen into a seedy almost abandoned area with X Rated movies. Through Mitchell Historical Properties, 1860's and the Wall Street of the South was recovered by restoring the outside facades while turning the interiors into condo's, law and real-estate offices and of course tourist businesses.

The Tremont, the elegant hotel with its rooftop bar overlooking the wharves is a destination stay for sure. Jazz soothes from the old bar out into the streets. Today, the half square mile area is the site for many events during the year, from Dickens on the Square to Mardi Gras. Seven million folks visit Galveston each year, largely due to the hometown boy's efforts.

Mitchell knew the rich and famous, yet avoided publicity — a shy man. This great read allows us to know the multifaceted man who changed history.

George P. Mitchell: Fracking, Sustainability and an Unorthodox Quest to Save the Planet, Texas A&M Press, 2019 by Loren C. Steffy

Hermits on SS Selma
By Bill Cherry

He changed his shirt with the same frequency that he changed his tattoos. That he was a hermit was more the result of his hygiene than that he didn't care to be around people.

Those who knew him called him Frenchy. His parents had named him Clesmey N. LeBlanc. The average person on the Island referred to him as the "crazy hermit" who lives on the concrete ship.

Christie "the Beachcomber" Mitchell, whose powerful exclamation to everyone was, "Baby, I'm going to make you a star," was the most creative publicist the island ever had. He decided he could bring nationwide notoriety to Galveston by making Frenchy a star.

Frenchy lived on the *SS Selma*, a ship that had been sunk in a water trench six feet deep off the coast of Pelican Island. It remains there today.

The SS *Selma* was one of twelve concrete ships the government decided to build during World War I to conserve steel. They were built on the east coast and to be oil tankers. They cost about $2 million each.

On its maiden voyage, the *Selma* went to Tampico. As it was arriving, its captain got off course and drove the boat over a jetty, puncturing its bottom, and causing its hold to fill with water, and the vessel to go aground.

Planks were nailed to the bottom as a temporary patch. She was then bailed out and towed to Galveston's Pier 35 for permanent repairs. A hurricane came into the gulf, and the *Selma's* new captain, Edward Howell, moved the ship under its own power to a safer place, Pier 10.

Some months later, in 1923, marine engineers concluded that she could not be repaired to be seaworthy. Again Capt. Howell fired-up the boat's steam engines, and moved her to her final resting place where she was run aground.

In 1947, Frenchy LeBlanc bought the *SS Selma*. LeBlanc paid its then owner, Henry Dalehite's Galvez Boat Service, one hundred bucks for it.

Frenchy, whose only teeth were those that had been given him by Dr. W.L. Glenn, Sr., had a bad leg which kept him from getting a good, full-time job. There was no welfare or public assistance of consequence in those days, and there was no permanent public subsidized housing. Frenchy decided that with his impairment, he could no longer afford high rent, women, taxes, or food from the grocery store, and he was certain no one was going to provide them free for him.

He decided that his best option was to buy the *Selma*. He could live in its cabin, fish from its deck, raise a goat or two and a handful of chickens on board, and sell day-passes to those who were curious about him, and who wanted to fish there. The enterprise worked.As the ferry boats passed, the passengers saw Frenchy fishing off of the ship's deck. They'd wave. Sometimes he'd wave back; other times he wouldn't. The ferry-boat deck-hands were certain that if you saw Frenchy wave, he was waving at the porpoises that were rolling above the water; he wasn't waving at you.

In the Indian Summer of 1947, Christie Mitchell was the public relations person for the Greater Galveston Beach Association. Looking for a publicity angle for the Island, he convinced Frenchy to found a bogus third political party—Happy Hermits. The club's first national convention would be held on the deck of the *Selma*, and the delegates would sit on three wash-tubs, four oyster crates and some makeshift driftwood benches. Their primary business would be to elect their own United States presidential candidate.

Large, cloth two-man banners on poles were made so they could be held up by the conventioneers for the ferry passengers to read: "We seek solution from intrusion." "Civilization? We'll stay in Galveston!" "We need women delegates. All applicants preapproved."

While Mitchell's claim was that the club members and convention delegates were hermit lifestyle sympathizers from Florida, Colorado, Maine, Michigan, New York, Arizona and elsewhere in Texas, in reality, they were his regular drinking buddies from Johnny Jack's club in the Marine Building on 21st and Mechanic Street.

It's a fact that a couple of those "delegates" were other Galveston characters, Lionel Pellerin, for an example. He was the dapper, handsome and admired maître d' at the Balinese Room. Somehow Mitchell convinced Movietone News and Universal News that the whole "convention" was on the up-and-up—a true and serious news event, not a promotion gimmick. They sent cameras to film the occasion.

Back then, newsreels were shown before every movie. In the newsreel Happy Hermits segments, viewers saw the delegates holding the club's "platform" banners, then Frenchy declining the nomination to be the club's first presidential candidate. Then they saw resolution: Safety Santa then being nominated and unanimously winning his bid as the Happy Hermit's presidential candidate.

Lee Orr of Fox Movietone estimated that in excess of twenty million movie-goers learned about Galveston, the "Playground of the Southwest."

It's interesting to note that shortly before the first Happy Hermits national convention was organized, the U.S. Army Corps of Engineers gave Houston's Harrisburg Machine Co. a permit to board the *Selma*, stack lumber from another wrecked boat on her deck, and burn it. This was apparently done without Frenchy's permission.

Mitchell had helped Frenchy find an attorney, another character in his own right, a fellow named Michael Kustoff. Kustoff claimed to be a white Russian who, before he had immigrated to Galveston, had been a captain of the Cossacks.

The *Selma*, sans Frenchy, remains today in its final resting place. The *Selma* was owned by a former reporter for the *Galveston Daily News*, Pat Daniels. That is appropriate, since Daniels appears to be a character in his own right. Each year he held an on-land birthday party for the *Selma*. Entertainment for the guest was provided by a huge kazoo band.

The *Selma* remains, a bit beaten up by Hurricane Ike, it continues to host sharks, dolphins and tourist boats every hour. *Selma* can be seen from the deck of USS *Stewart* in the Galveston Naval Museum. Just look north, up the Houston ship channel.

SS Selma's bow after 100 years aground. The ferries pass aft every few minutes.

End Note: The parties moved to a large yard in the historic section of Galveston, as Daniels and his pals aged to walkers and wheel chairs. The last of the celebrations ended in the early 2000's.

Source: "*SS Selma, the Concrete ship, hosts the 1947 National Happy Hermits Political Convention*"; from Bill Cherry's book, *Bill Cherry's Galveston Memories*, 2000 VanJus Press, Galveston, Texas. (Used with permission; edited for space.)

CHAPTER 2
High Seas Adventures

In this Chapter
Sallee

High seas shipping is the term we use for the transportation for 90% of items moved on earth. Given that 70% of the earth is covered by water, passage by sea makes sense. It is cheap, if not quick, and usually without dangers.

Beyond ships, the most critical component of high seas shipping are the people who operate these complex huge machines. The process of getting aboard as a crew member and what it is like to experience life at sea in different roles is explained through author Mike Leahy's 45 years of encounters shared in several articles in this chapter. Author Alvin Sallee added his interviews with crew members on board ships or who visited the Galveston Seafarers Center.

Cargo conveyance by sea is the principal method of bringing us everything from autos to X-Ray machines, yet the whole process is little understood. Billions of dollars go into port communities' economies as the industry employs over a million people.

You can enjoy the voyage with your commodities and crewmembers in this chapter.

Bulk Cargo Ship Around the Cape
Sallee

"How long will your cruise to Tanzania be?" I asked.

"About five weeks around Cape of Good Hope," the crew member, Jerome, answered.

We were sitting on an "L" shaped green vinyl couch around a table in the crew's mess hall on the ship.

"Well this certainly is not a cruise liner," I commented. They all chuckled.

Drogba is a British owned bulk cargo carrier flagged and operated by a Singapore company.

"You don't go through the Suez Canal?" I asked.

"No."

"Does that save money?"

As matter of fact, yes, $465,000. And only a day longer.

For the crew, all from the Philippines, like 800,000 of their countrymen, the sea is a way of life--and increased income.

Chaplain Karen Parsons, of the Seafarers Center, has brought me aboard as part of her visitation ministry to crew members far from home on nine month long contracts. We spoke to the chief mate, the number two man in charge of the ship. Other crew members included deckhands, an engineman, the assistant cook and of course, the captain, known as the Ole' Man.

They ranged in experience from a 20-year-old on his first voyage to the Chief, Roberto, with 27 years. After ten years, Roberto took a two-year break, but his family could not afford the reduced income so he went back to sea. He has a son, majoring in psychology at a private university in St. Carlos. And his daughter, who after seven years will become a lawyer.

Karen asked, "Will she make a good living as an attorney in the Philippines?"

"I don't know," he answered. "But she loved to read. Ever since she was a young girl she selected the thickest book, not children's books." He beamed with pride. The kids' education came with a penalty—his absence for nine months out of the year.

With a master's license, he could become a captain of a cargo vessel. However, he wants to stay chief to gain more experience.

While we visited, the assistant cook brought sweet bread and water. He allowed me to make a cup of instant coffee, while not the MOD coffee shop, it wasn't bad. When he returned to the galley I whispered to Karen, "I wonder if they got this bread in New Orleans, the last stop?"

She answered, "No, it was made today on the ship."

Wow. Delicious, I would put on some pounds.

All of the crew were thin, so I remarked, "You must work hard not to put on weight." The cook laughed.

His hours are 6 a.m. to 6 p.m. seven days a week with a two-hour rest break from 1:00 to 3:00, a good tradition left by the Spanish.

Karen asked every crew member about their family. Each spoke with pride, and a bit of sadness, in their voice. Seafarers pay a high price for us to have low costs. They spend months apart with only rare Internet conversations with their family.

With US regulations, this crew could not get off the ship in Galveston. They could only stare at the wonderful community their labor provides us.

Visit a Seafarers Center sometime, and if you can't, send them some money.

Bulk carriers, such as Drogba here in Galveston Harbor, are often loaded in grain shot down in the holds off of conveyer belts from dock side silos.

A Pierhead Jump
Michael Leahy

The first time I caught a deep-sea ship it was a pierhead jump. I joined her about an hour before sailing and I was schooner-rigged. The ship was a break-bulk steam freighter of Lykes Brothers Line, then one of the largest of the American liner companies, with 43 freighters in their fleet. The ship was at the city docks in Houston and the sailing board was posted for 1800 hours when someone realized that the 12-4 ordinary seaman had failed to turn to for his afternoon watch.

He had gone ashore in the morning, gotten drunk and was passed out in his fo'c'sle. The mate and bo'sn shook him out of his rack, stuffed his gear in his seabag and dragged him up to the Old Man's office to get paid off, then escorted him down the gangway. Meanwhile, the Old Man had to go out to the telephone booth on the dock, call the Lykes' home office in New Orleans and request that a new ordinary be called, hopefully before the ship sailed.

The company's personnel manager in New Orleans then called the union headquarters in New York, which in turn called the union hall in Houston. They got the job onto the shipping board at 1600 hours, just in time for the last job call of the day.

That's how those things were accomplished back then.

In 1972, the huge surge in shipping caused by the Vietnam War was beginning to slow. From approximately 1965 until then, the sealift for Vietnam had many of the commercial liner company ships on Military Sealift Command (MSC) charter. Many of the WWII-era freighters that had been mothballed in the National Reserve Fleet were activated as well. All these support vessels for the war effort were manned by civilian merchant mariners, as has been the case in every armed conflict of the United States since the inception of the Merchant Marine in 1775. Any breathing man with a Z-Card (merchant mariner document) could ship out anytime he wanted, and sometimes even if he didn't. Ships returning from Vietnam often experienced a suitcase brigade among the unlicensed crewmembers as soon as they docked in a U.S. port.

This occurred for two reasons:

One: In those days, crews signed on for normally no less than six-month foreign articles in the presence of a shipping commissioner, often even for 12-month articles. But the articles would be broken, and a full payoff conducted by law if the ship returned to a U.S. port. The seamen could then quit the ship without penalties and with their full pay due in cash.

Two: With the war bonus being paid while in Vietnamese waters, and the typical freighter remaining in port or at anchor there for weeks every voyage, they had a whole lot of money coming to them (again, in cash ...), and they knew they could catch another ship as soon as they ran out of money.

The need to fill out enough crew to at least enable the vessel to get underway sometimes even caused union officials to go to bars nearest their union halls, drag union members right off their bar stools, hand them shipping cards that had already been filled out, and drive them down to the ship. This was ironic, as they were for all intents and purposes Shanghai'g their own members. One of the main reasons these seamen's unions were organized, and union officials had fought hard to get the Seamen's Act of 1915 passed through the US Congress, was to stop this very practice of Shanghai'g by the old crimps and boarding masters.

Often, some seamen in such a waterfront bar had already gone through all their last payoff and were drinking and often eating and sleeping by means of a tab being run by the bar owner. These tabs were the first bill paid off by the seamen upon their return and payoff from a voyage, to ensure their credit would remain good in the future. So, when the union representatives came in looking for seamen to fill out the crew of a ship about to get underway, the bar owner was quick to point out those men who were running up a tab, as it was in his own best interest to get them working again. In any case, during the war it was no problem to get a berth, even if a seaman had low seniority and limited endorsements.

While Merchant Marine ships continued to sail for Vietnam until the final withdrawal in 1975, the sealift began to wind down sooner with the peace talks and lead up to the cease fire. This led to fewer berths available so, having seniority with the union, as well as multiple endorsements so more than one position on a ship was available to you, started to make a big difference in how long a seaman might find himself stuck on the beach. Those without either could be waiting a long time to get a berth. When they did, it was usually only because no one else wanted the job, for any number of reasons

Author Leahy, standing between SS Cove Leader main engine turbines on the 25,000-horsepower tanker. Photo courtesy of Leahy.

In the case of my pierhead jump, the job call came in so close to the last call of the day that most of the seamen in the hall who were eligible to throw in on that ordinary's job had concluded that there would be no more jobs on the board that day. They had already headed across the street to Betty's, a decrepit old bar run by the wife of a chief steward. While they enjoyed cold Pearl beers, I scored the job because I was still lurking around the back of the union hall. That is how a young seaman with only entry ratings and lacking a full union book scored a berth at that time. A combination of luck and ... maybe a little *baksheesh* to a union patrolman might have helped too.

As said earlier, I also joined this ship schooner-rigged. This means I had no time to go home and get my gear. (One is said to join a ship schooner-rigged when one has only the clothing one is wearing and no gear whatsoever, even a toothbrush.) If a ship is sailing foreign, this is not much of a problem since toiletries, work clothes and underwear, cigarettes, candy etc. are available on credit against wages earned (but held by the company) from the ship's slop chest. However, since this ship was in the middle of the coastwise portion of her voyage, hitting next several U.S. ports in the Gulf Mexico, the slop chest was locked and sealed by U.S. Customs. This was because all slop chest goods are purchased by the company and sold to the seamen duty-free.

Fortunately, by late the next day we were docked at Lyke's Bros. main homeport at the Nashville Wharf in New Orleans. I had enough money in my pocket to go ashore and buy a few items to carry me through, plus get a spaghetti dinner at Frankie and Johnnie's. The ship's coastwise voyage plan had her going next to Mobile, then Pensacola, then back to Galveston where I could pick up my seabag from my flop.

When I'd caught the ship back at Houston, the word I was given by the union agent was that the ship would complete the coastwise cargo discharging portion of her most recent voyage to various African ports, and then go on MSC charter to take a full load to Vietnam. This was also the word amongst the officers and crew onboard. However, while making our way among the various U.S. Gulf Coast ports on her itinerary this plan changed, as is often the case in the life of seamen. Instead, another Lyke's ship made the Southeast Asia trip and I soon found myself on an 18-day sea passage from New Orleans to Cape Town, South Africa, with a preliminary call at Walvis Bay in Southwest Africa (now called Namibia). From Cape Town, we spent a couple of months calling in and out of East Africa ports such as East London, Durban, Lourenco Marques, Beira, Tanga, and Mombasa. Finally, we made a 30-day sea passage from Mombasa back to New Orleans.

Everyone's first deep-sea trip should include passage around the Cape of Good Hope. Twice, I got the experience of sailing in 65-foot seas and greater (in good weather, not a storm!) under my belt early on, and joined the Equator Club on that voyage as well. Once learning that seas that huge are just another day at sea when rounding Agulhas, I seldom encountered sea conditions that caused me any distress for the rest of my 24 years as a seaman.

Seafarer Exploitation
Sallee

> *"There is nothing more enticing, disenchanting, and enslaving than the life at sea."*
>
> —*Lord Jim*, Joseph Conrad

The sea has been a prime site for exploitation, from 1500 BC Phoenician slave-rowed boats, through ships of today. Seafarers, sailors, often pay an unseen price in our world of cruise and cargo ships. The *Golden Ray,* tied up at the Galveston wharf comes to mind. Away from family for months, isolated, with little social interaction while employed in a largely unregulated industry. Coming mostly from former colonies, seafarers easily can serve as cogs in the wheels of the maritime business.

Golden Ray, at pier 39, is a 659-foot-long ship with a crew's lounge 30-feet wide, a small living quarters for 28 Filipino crew members, each with separate cabins. The small group rarely get off the ship over their nine month contracts, thanks in part to U.S. regulations.

U.S. immigration allows a 29-day period to visit our ports even though they have been screened. This crew spent almost two weeks in New Orleans waiting for the load. They were able to get off only one day. A week sailing, and another waiting off Galveston for the grain to arrive. Twenty-nine days expired, so the crew wasn't allowed off. Unable to use the internet, spend money at the box stores, or pick up packages, they could only stand at the rail and look across the wharf into our town.

In 2015 there were 1.6 million seafarers, led by the Philippines and Indonesia. The Russian Federation, Ukraine and India rounded out the top five. China's seafarers have limited international roles.

Many international crew members can be found aboard cruise ships which host millions of seagoing U.S. citizens each year, looking for a bargain. Cruising is a big industry.

Cruise line companies reported 2018 yearly profits as: Carnival, $3.2 billion; Royal Caribbean, $1.8 billion; and Norwegian, $954.8 million.

Their employees' median salaries for long hours were: Norwegian, $20,101; Royal Caribbean, $19,396; and Carnival, $16,622.

CEO pay: Norwegian, Frank Del Rio: $22,593,061 (that is $22.5 million dollars); Carnival, Arnold Donald: $13,515,884; and Royal Caribbean, Richard Fain: $12,422,715.

Exploitation is treating someone unfairly in order to benefit from their work. CEOs make over 1,000 times more than an average worker. Unfair?

Number of employees for each company: Carnival, 154,161; Royal Caribbean, 77,000; and Norwegian, 33,200. Yes, this will be on the final exam.

We should appreciate the largely unknown people who play such critical sea related roles in our community. Seafarers need friends in ports of call.

In Galveston, the friend since 1839 has been the Seafarers Center located in the 1870's John Kobbel Building. Bought by the Moody Foundation in 1977, it's located on 20th Street, just steps from busy wharves.

Chaplain Karen Parsons, Kimberly Hall, Denise Hightower-Aguilar and volunteers "humanize" seafarers who place themselves in jeopardy for weeks at a time on the high seas transporting bananas to wind turbines, to provide for their families. On these vessels are fathers, brothers, uncles, and sons, mothers, sisters and daughters who labor far from home and look to the Center as a place of respite and reconnection."

To get involved: *galvestonseafarerscenter.org*

The Banana Boat
Sallee

"Want bananas?" I asked. It was 6:00 a.m. at HEB grocery store.

"Yes, if can you find some green ones," came cook Mike Morin's reply.

"Maybe I could pick some up when I go aboard the banana boat today. Ha!"

Later that day, 1300 hours, I climbed the gangway behind Chaplain Karen Parsons, up many stories, through several doors to a bare mess hall lined with safety posters around one window.

We missed the lunch crowd.

A 30-year-old t-shirt clad man, James, came out of the galley smiling, "May I get you something to drink? Coffee, water or juice?"

Karen asked for water, I juice. A moment later he reappeared with glasses full of ice. "Sorry we only have mango."

"Great, my favorite," I disclosed.

He smiled broadly. "It's our favorite juice in the Philippines."

We were in the crew's mess hall aboard MV *Star*, the refrigerated "Banana Boat". (Ironically, it is known as bad luck if a seafarer eats a banana on a ship. I guess they might slip on the peel?) A poster on the drab green bulkhead (wall) proclaimed English as the official working language.

James remembered Karen from a big birthday party last month. He asked her if she got the photos through "messenger." After searching through her phone, she could not find them. Asking for her phone James quickly found the landscape photo of 21 happy crew members sitting behind a table full of food.

The Seafarers Center had received a gift of six nice wrist watches. What do you do with six presents and 21 crew members? You hold a raffle. The birthday boy won one watch and great fun was had by all.

The faces in that photograph beamed broadly with eyes laughing. A break that day from stressful jobs these men hold.

The sea is a dangerous place to work. Seaman being helivac'd from offshore of Corpus Christi, TX, after fatal injury during lifeboat drill. His skull was crushed by a winch crank handle when the lifeboat stuck in the davits, then dropped by gravity. Photo by Leahy.

In order for me to get bananas they must arrive in Galveston at 11:00 p.m. every Sunday night. One day in Santo Tomas, Guatemala, two and a half days across part of the Caribbean Sea and all of the Gulf of Mexico, a day in Galveston, and begin all over again. Week after week. Month after month.

James had just completed three of his nine-month contract. Before this contract he was off for 10 months. His family owns a rice farm where he works between ships. He enjoys it but it doesn't pay.

I sip my mango juice as James and Karen chat like old friends. The fire at Notre Dame in Paris. His aunt lives there doing domestic work. His family in Houston wants him to come to the U.S. to live. He would only be able to go home every three years. On the ship he goes home every nine months and the company pays his way.

And he really likes his home in the Philippines.

A relative who captains a ferry in the Philippines wants James to get certified so he could be a cook's assistant on the ferry but it pays less.

Then there is money. James is an economic expert on money exchanges. Today it was 52 pesos to $1 U.S. When Karen visited the Philippines in 2000 it was 33 pesos to $1.

Almost an hour has slipped by. James has had an energized conversation with someone who cares. An oasis for this young man at sea.

A Day in the Life, At Sea
Leahy

Engine Department Officer: *The second engineer on a steamship is responsible for the main propulsion boilers, in addition to his normal watch-standing duties for the entire ship's plant. Typically, the 2nd takes the 4 to 8 watch (0400-0800 and 1600-2000) each day. This watch schedule enables him to work the most overtime hours on maintenance and repairs to his boilers. And, should he actually get a chance to go ashore while the ship is in port, it leaves the best hours open to do so.*

0330 (3:30 a.m.)
The oiler from the 12-4 watch bangs on the 2nd's stateroom door to wake him for watch. Having had about six hours of sleep, he rolls out of his bunk, uses the head, then steps into the clean boiler suit hanging on a nearby hook. He stuffs a pair of clean socks in his front pocket and pulls on his boots over bare feet. Snatching up his flashlight, channel locks, and aluminum cigarette case, he is ready for work. He exits his stateroom, walks across the passageway to the engine room casing door, and enters his workspace.

Still more asleep than awake, he drops down the ladders to the throttle platform to relieve the 12-4 third engineer. He listens as the 3rd advises him of any unusual circumstances with the plant or ship movements. (Sometimes he'll even hear what the 3rd is saying.) Second (2nd) engineers usually have the pick of the best oiler, so he'll send his oiler out to make the first round of the engine room, fire room and other machinery spaces.

Quickly scanning critical gauges and thermometers on the main gauge board at the throttles, he ensures the plant is stable. His eyes go first to the water level indicators for the boilers. Then he checks the steam pressure and superheated steam temperature from the boilers and pressure at the inlet to the first stage of the high-pressure turbine of the main engine. This is such second nature for him, he records the position of the various needles and levels as either okay or seriously wrong subconsciously. It takes his oiler twenty minutes to complete his round, visually checking all local gauges, thermometers, liquid levels of water and lubes. Meanwhile he puts the back of his hand on all the electric motors and bearings of rotating machinery to be sure they're not running hot.

Now the 2nd can get the first of the many cups of coffee he'll drink during his watch. He sits on a rung of the ladder extending from the decks above to remove his boots, put on the socks he'd earlier stuffed in his pockets, and pull his boots back on. By now he's fully awake and has been listening closely to the sound of the plant. While it's at a level considered deafening to an outsider, to the engineer it's sending a clear message of "all's well" or "something's not right." He goes back over each of the gauges and thermometers on the main board again, this time noting their precise reading and checking the less critical ones as well. Finally, he reviews the log book entries for the prior two watches. While he's been asleep, every single detail of every piece of machinery in the plant has been noted.

When the oiler returns—assuming he has nothing untoward to report from his rounds—the 2nd is relieved from his standby position at the main board/throttles/log desk/phone booth. He retires to the fire room, third cup of coffee in hand. It's time to test the boiler water chemistry.

Behind the boilers there's a stainless-steel sink with a small, high-pressure pipe leading from each boiler's steam and water drum through a cooler. This condenses the steam to water that's cool enough to be handled. Above the sink is a cabinet filled with test chemicals and assorted laboratory appliances for testing the chemistry of the water in the boilers.

Over time, even a tightly maintained condensing steam plant will have a gradual increase in chlorides (salts), so the level must be monitored. When it gets too high, the boiler(s) must be blown down and additional feed water replenished to them. Feed water, coming from evaporators converting salt water to distilled water, will normally not exceed one-quarter of a grain per gallon of chlorides. The chemistry is also checking for the boiler water's acidity/alkalinity.

After logging his findings, the 2nd determines the amount of treatment chemicals he needs to inject into the boilers to maintain proper balance. Water chemistry is extremely critical in boilers operating near 850 lbs. per square inch pressure and 900° Fahrenheit steam temperature at the outlet of the super-heaters. Chlorides or other solids in suspension can adhere to the inside of the boiler tubes. This prevents free flow of heat from the fireside to the water side of the thousands of tubes in the boiler, and results in overheating the tube's metal and a boiler blow out. Checking, and if necessary, dosing the boiler with treatment chemicals to correct its chemistry is of the 2nd's most important daily tasks. If something seriously wrong is detected, such as a spike in chloride level indicating a saltwater leak in the main condenser or elsewhere in the plant, more elaborate steps may have to be taken.

0600 (6 a.m.)

Mid-watch, the 2nd makes a full round of all the machinery spaces, carefully observing the proper operation of all elements of the plant. If he doesn't have a sharp and reliable oiler, he's likely make more than one full round himself, just to be on the safe side. In the last hour of the watch, the oiler will make what's known as his "reading" round. This is when he records all the temperatures and pressure/vacuum reading, tank levels and other pertinent data of the steam plant locally (as opposed to the remote repeater gauges at the throttle platform). These figures will be used by the 2nd to fill out the engine room logbook, which is done in great detail. The 2nd also takes a one-minute reading of the main propeller shaft revolutions per minute. This he does by visual observation of the turning shaft, not by relying on any RPM meter.

0745 (7:45 a.m.)

The 3rd engineer (8-12) comes below and relieves the 2nd. His first watch of the day is over, and it's time to go above for breakfast in the officer's saloon. While he eats, he'll likely talk with the chief and first engineer about the state of his boilers and his plans for the day. After breakfast, the 2nd goes back below for maintenance and repair work on his boilers.

A good 2nd always has a couple of boiler gauge glass units overhauled, rebuilt, and ready to be installed if a gauge glass blows out. And he's always in the process of rebuilding boiler soot blowers, continually swapping a rebuilt one for another one to work on. He conducts never-ending maintenance and repairs on boiler ancillary equipment, burner management and combustion control automation components, fuel oil burners and system components, and steam turbine-driven feed pumps. It's a constant process.

1000 (10 a.m.)

Coffee with the 1st and 3rd in the fire room, instead of going above to the saloon for just 15-20 minutes. *Note:* Coffee time, occurring each day at 1000 and 1500, is a sacrosanct ritual observed by every member of the crew, top to bottom, deck or engine. A common way to praise the long experience and skills of a seaman of any rank or department is to say that he has more "coffee time" than anyone else has "sea time." This is similar to the expression: "I have passed more lighthouses than you have passed telephone poles."

1130 (11:30 a.m.)

Time to go up above, clean up, grab some lunch, then try for a 30-minute nap on the settee or recliner in his stateroom.

1300 (1:00 p.m.)

Maintenance work continues below until coffee time. This time the 2nd returns to the saloon or goes on deck for fresh sea air before relieving the 12-4 watch.

1545 (3:45 p.m.)

Evening watch is similar to morning, except that right after the oiler's first round it's time for the daily blowing of tubes in the boilers. The 2nd engineer alerts the 2nd mate on watch on the bridge, then he slows the ship. Slowing the ship reduces steam to the main engine enough to accommodate the steam lost in the tube blowing process. Soot blowers are large alloy steel lances inserted into the fireside of the boiler superheater and generating tube banks and the uptakes. Their purpose is to blow accumulating soot from the firesides of the boilers out the top of the stack. This prevents the accumulation of soot from interfering with heat exchange across the boiler tubes, which would otherwise result in tube failure and boiler casualty.

It takes 30-40 minutes to blow tubes, then the 2nd settles the boilers and plant down, and brings the ship back up to full sea speed. The last step is a call to the bridge to confirm to the 2nd mate that they are up to full sea speed and the plant is settled. These calls to the bridge are logged in the bridge logbook as well. If the 2nd is in the habit of eating dinner, one of the 3rds comes down to relieve him just long enough to go above and eat. (Not everyone enjoys their dinner bookended by a couple of hours in a hot engine room, so many times the 2nd will just skip it.)

1945 (7:45 p.m.)

The 3rd comes down to begin the 8-12 watch. The 2nd now goes up to perhaps have a beer or two in the chief's office, a chance to talk over the events of the day with the chief and first engineer.

2030 (8:30 p.m.)

The 2nd heads for his stateroom to take a shower and "put it on the padded shelf" (go to bed, in shoreside terms).

0330 (3:30 a.m. next morning)

The call comes to start the entire process all over again. A typical 2nd Engineer works a schedule of approximately 14-hour days for seven days a week and four-month tours of duty. He may get opportunities to go ashore while in port during those four months, but since often there's work on the boilers that can only be safely done while docked, time ashore is not a guarantee. For this he is well paid and earns day-for-day vacation. However, the salary he earns while on vacation is base salary only. Without all the overtime hours, vacation pay is quite a bit less than pay while at sea.

Note: A second engineer can usually be immediately identified by looking at his hands and forearms. His fingertips are stained black from the silver nitrate used each day testing boiler water. And his forearms, just above the wrists, usually have burn scars in the gap between the gauntlet of his gloves and boiler-suit cuffs, a result of extending his arms while working on a hot boiler.

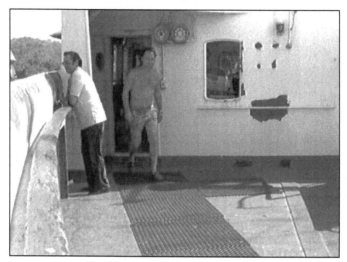

Captain Jack Flanagan exits the bridge of a tanker transiting the Panama Canal.
The lead pilot is leaning on the spray dodger at left.
Clearly, informal dress is allowed on tankers. Photo courtesy of Leahy.

Fourth Arm of Defense
Sallee

If you have any doubts about the next generation, just spend a day with the Texas A&M--Galveston cadets. Having worked around college students my whole career I am impressed each time they visit the Galveston Naval Museum. Students complete class assignments in ship maintenance and mooring with USS Stewart's working capstan lowering and raising the anchor. And they are great workers on cleanup during volunteer days. After graduation, a few go into the United States Navy but most will try to join the U.S. Merchant Marine as Navy Reservists.

The Merchant Marine is critical for our national security. Only U.S. flagged ships can transport U.S. troops and supplies to combat areas. The U.S. company owned vessels, which carry cargo during peace time, become part of the Defense Department during conflicts.

As Mike Leahy experienced during Desert Storm in the Middle East, ammunition, helicopters, troops and all their supplies traveled on U.S. flagged vessels. And as Mike has told me, all Mariners serving on the U.S. flagged ships take an oath to the United States to serve during wartime. Which is all well and good except there is a shortage of people and ships.

Col. Michael Fossum, the Chief Operating Officer and Vice President at Texas A&M--Galveston has shared with me the challenges of recruiting students to the Maritime Academy at A&M, one of only seven in the United States. For this group of new workers this is not an 8 to 5 job.

As Sarah Scherer, Director and Associate Dean at the Community College, Seattle Maritime Academy (not one of the seven) stated regarding this new generation, "This millennial generation has never been disconnected. They don't know what it's like to be separated from friends and family and they are the ones we are trying to recruit."

On many ships there is no internet, you can't stream data and you aren't going to stay in touch using your cell phone. As a result, we'd like to recruit people who have traveled or been in the military and might be more prepared for that kind of separation.

When graduates return to visit us at the Galveston Naval Museum I often hear about the long time at sea being a difficult barrier, especially for this generation accustomed to constant connection over the Internet and cell phones. They begin at the bottom of the rung, spending long hours in the engine rooms or as an able body seaman. And while their trips provide adventure, Merchant Marine jobs must compete with lucrative, more stable jobs ashore.

Laura Elder wrote in a *Galveston Daily News* editorial, "A severe maritime labor shortage threatens more than industry and commerce, it's a national security threat that we all have a vested interest in rectifying. The U.S. Merchant Marine fleet has declined from 1,288 international trading vessels in 1951 to 81 today." *(Dec. 10, 2019)*

Col. Fossum strongly supports A&M cadets engaging in hands-on work at the Galveston Naval Museum. To meet one of the largest challenges, the fact that many young students don't know anything about the maritime industry and its opportunities, the Galveston Naval Museum has put together a Shipmates Program to bring school children to the vessels for STEAM Science, Technology mini-classes and sleep overs.

Once students know about the industry, they have to be willing to rise to the demands of professionalism and, for some positions, spend many weeks at sea. The students I have stayed in touch with, who went to sea, so far have gone on to fulfilling careers in the Marchant Maine.

As Elder concluded, "U.S. Merchant Marine graduates and other maritime industry workers play key roles in an industry vital to the US economy and continued prosperity. But they also serve the nation as the "fourth arm of defense" in times of conflict." In Chapter 8, author Mike Leahy puts a personal face to this commitment.

Staying in Touch at Sea
Leahy

When I hear that prospective candidates to become future seamen, whether officers or crew, are inhibited by the inconvenience of not being connected to the Internet and having cell phone service 24/7, I have to reflect upon what personal communication was like in the years when I went to sea and for many years prior to that. In reality, their anticipated isolation is today, far from as complete as perhaps they imagine. Many ships today have unlimited, or at least somewhat limited access to the Internet and e-mail for crew members, and anytime the ship is reasonably close to a populated area of land, crewmembers' cell phone will work. On a coastwise voyage, one is not often out of cell phone range.

Up until the early 1990s there were no such things as individual cell phones or e-mail. Communications with family and friends at home had several options for the average seafarer during a typical four month or greater time aboard ship. Some seamen chose to remain with a ship indefinitely and could be aboard much longer than this. For freighters sailing foreign on well established runs, each seaman was provided with a list of the company's agents in each port on the itinerary and this could be used by the seaman's communicants to send him letters while he was overseas. Seaman could, in turn, write letters back home and send them via the company's agent when the ship came to a port.

It was possible, albeit challenging, to go ashore and make a collect international telephone call from some ports, using hotels or telephone exchanges. This could prove impossible in many small ports of the undeveloped world.

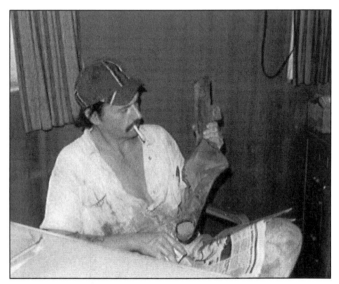

Author Leahy, inspecting a section of blown out main boiler screen tube in chief's office aboard SS Cove Mariner. Photo courtesy of Leahy.

For ships sailing coastwise in the U.S., or returning to a U.S. port from foreign, there was usually a telephone booth at the end of the dock where a seaman could place a collect call home. Of course, this public pay telephone, often just one, would be used by every member of the crew (sometimes members of several ships' crews) who lined up to take a turn. The ship's captain and chief engineer would also be using the same public telephone to call the home office and conduct other ship business. One of my favorite locations for calling home from the dock was at the Alyeska oil terminal at Valdez, Alaska because of the danger of bear attacks.

The terminal had built small, heated shacks at the head of the two piers with a pay phone inside and no crew were permitted to walk anywhere except from the gangway to the shack, lest they become a bear's dinner. You could not stand outside to provide some privacy to a shipmate inside calling home, for the same reason.

Also, anyone wanting to go ashore and into town must call the one taxi in Valdez to come and pick him up from the same phone and so, a trip to town could be delayed for as long as however many crew members before you had however long a call they needed to have with their home, which was likely to be the first call in anywhere from two weeks to two months, depending on what run the ship was on from Valdez. It was also not uncommon to have to remain in the shack indefinitely, if a large bear decided to come by and see if he could get to the people inside.

Communications at sea took place via Morse code from a shore radio station to the ship's radio operator. This was normally restricted to telegrams sent to and from the ship's home office and the charterers and, of course were kept short and terse. Individual crewmembers and their families ashore almost never communicated in this way while the ship was at sea but, it was possible to do so. A family member could call or go to their local Western Union office and dictate a short message which would be relayed to a shore radio station and then onward to the ship at sea.

This was expensive and difficult and was therefore usually reserved only for the most urgent of family news and that was generally very bad news. To have the word passed that a seafarer needed to go up to the radio shack because the radio operator had a message from home for him was usually a notice of death of a loved one ashore, and therefore no one really wanted to be told there was a message for him.

By the early 1990s, ships had begun to have satellite telephone communications, and this too was very expensive, starting at $10 USD per minute. The captains and chiefs were generally happy with this arrangement as it made communications right from their office desks with the company and charterers easier, and the company paid the bill. A public telephone provided by the satellite telephone company was also put onboard many ships for the use of the crewmembers.

Typically, it was mounted in the radio shack. If they had a credit card to charge the call to and were prepared to pay $100 for a ten-minute call with no privacy, a crew member could call home anytime the radio operator was on duty.

I sailed with a chief who found a way to have long communication with his wife at minimal cost under these conditions. He would write a lengthy letter to his wife and, using the captain's photocopier, reduce it to the smallest size, so that he could put a four-page letter on one page. Then he used the captain's fax machine to send the single page via the satellite telephone to his home phone number. This was only a one or two-minute satellite connection for what would have otherwise been a 20 or 30-minute verbal phone call.

Author Leahy, with his mother, Jeanne Leahy, on board SS Cove Liberty, a tanker at anchor at Colon, Panama. Photo courtesy of Leahy.

Where there is will, there is a way. The fact is that the world has always been divided into two very different groups of people: those who go to sea and those who remain ashore. The manifold differences in the temperaments, personalities, and indeed the entire lives of these two groups of people would itself fill a book and communications ashore while at sea is but one of the issues.*

Some people are born to be seafarers; most are not. Anyone who fears that a few days without internet and cell phone connection would be a problem is not going to adapt to the hundreds of other differences in the life of a seafarer, and so they should not look to pursue such a career in the first place.

*Note: Indeed, it has filled a book. See: Seamen Ashore: A Study of the United Seamen's Service and of Merchant Seamen in Port, by Elmo Hohman. (Available through online booksellers.)

Seafarers at Christmas
Sallee

Dusk has just passed. From Seawall and 45th Street I count thirty-three lights on the sea. Almost 2,300 souls waiting off Galveston to come into port.

This holiday season 1.2 million seafarers will be at sea, including 700,000 from the Philippines. Sailors live on the margins of society, mostly beyond the reach of land. It is a life of isolation away from families. Ships do not take vacations. Sailors are on a four-hour watch, off eight hours, on a voyage lasting months.

Meanwhile on land, from Halloween to Christmas Eve, every store is packed with tons of potential gifts. Yet, the sailors who bring the presents thousands of miles themselves often go without even one gift.

This holiday, at least 1,000 sailors off Galveston will receive a shoe box of gifts through the Galveston Seafarers Center, 221 20th Street. Houston will distribute 10,000 boxes. As Rick Cousins wrote in *The Daily News*, Galveston is home of the remarkable Chaplain Karen Parsons, the driving force behind the shoe boxes.

Afraid of heights and the sea, this woman climbs six stories on a swinging gangway up the side of the ships in port to deliver the gifts.

One year, on the "Banana Boat" ship, the crew of Ukraine and Russian sailors slowly unwrapped their shoe boxes, careful not to tear the paper. After looking at the small gifts of personal items, drawings by children and postcards, they rewrapped the boxes still in awe. When asked why, they said they wanted their families to experience opening the present too. They could not believe that strangers would give them presents.

Pan Viva crew members hand out some of the wrapped shoe box Christmas presents in the ward room. Author Sallee and Kathy Sallee look on.

Another Christmas, a ship caught fire and two sailors died. The crew was mostly from the Philippines. While the investigation went on aboard ship, the crew was housed at the La Quinta on the seawall. The crew grieved the loss of their friends. They were allowed to dine at Denny's, but their main staple, rice, was not on the menu. Chaplain Parsons to the rescue, or should I say, kitchen.

Like Chaplain Karen, women make up less than two percent of sailors on merchant ships and 18 percent on cruise ships. Sexual harassment is a major problem for women who work in regular seafarer jobs. One woman in the engineering department shaved her head and dressed as a man to protect herself.

One study indicated that the presence of women on the crew reduced the feeling of isolation and thus could reduce turnover in the crew. The main reason given for crew not shipping out again is missing their family.

On our dining room table, we put together 25 plastic shoe boxes. Postcards, holiday towels, personal items, Santa hat and hand written cards wishing the sailor a peaceful holiday season. Five stores later, and an aching back we are finished.

How does Chaplain Parsons pack 1000? Probably one at a time. If you would like to help, contact the center at (409)762-0655.

Somehow I feel closer to the sailors, miles from shore.

The Jones Act
Leahy

An often-asked question by cruise ship customers is, "Why can't we go from one U.S. city port to another without going to another country?" The answer lies with the Passenger Vessel Services Act, passed by Congress in 1886 and providing for such restrictions on foreign ships carrying U.S. passengers between U.S. locations. For context, "Why can't we go from one U.S. city to another on Lufthansa, Cathay Pacific or British Airways? Domestic air travel is also restricted to U.S. owned and manned carriers.

But the real importance of the Passenger Vessel Services Act lies with its relationship to its "sister act": The Merchant Marine Act of 1920, commonly called the Jones Act, after its congressional sponsor. Both are cabotage laws that control access to U.S. shipping markets by foreign entities. Few Americans have any real understanding of either law, but it is the Jones Act that provides critical national security support for every American citizen.

Powerful lobbyists for multinational agribusiness and petroleum interests have long waged war on the Jones Act, and any attempt to gain support for repeal of passenger ship cabotage restrictions is but a wedge under the door for repeal of the Jones Act. In addition to establishing employment and safe working condition rights for U.S. merchant seamen, it is a law reserving ocean-borne ship trade between American ports for U.S. flag ships, owned by American companies, built in American shipyards, and crewed by American citizens.

For those with narrow vision, it can be viewed as a "protectionist" law, benefiting a small segment of the U.S. population (those in the maritime industry). But the truth is that the Jones Act has been for the last century, and remains, critically important to every American man, woman, and child, whether they are seamen from Maine or farmers from Iowa.

My family has been in the maritime business—sailing, building, and repairing ships—for four generations now. The last three generations have been in the United States, where we participated in every war and armed conflict from WWII to Operation Iraqi Freedom II. The Jones Act can fairly be said to be responsible for feeding, housing, and educating all of those last three generations of productive, tax-paying citizens. We have over one hundred calendar years of experience in two countries and, if multiplied by the number of individual family members in the industry, that experience level is more like two hundred years.

But how does the Jones Act help to feed, house, and educate not just our family but every family in America, regardless of what businesses they are in or in what part of our large country they live? The answer lies in the security that has enabled every one of us to live in a free country where, when our military must go to war, it does so far from our shores.

When the U.S. commits to armed conflicts overseas, a massive sealift is required to move all the equipment required to conduct war a few thousand miles from our shores. Everything from tomahawk missiles and jet fuel for those stealth bombers to Humvees, Bradley Fighting Vehicles and M1-Abrams tanks, goes on U.S. ships manned by civilian American officers and crewmembers. For Desert Storm for example, we broke out 80 former commercial freighters and tankers from the National Defense Reserve Fleet, sometimes called the "mothball fleet", to provide all munitions and all other cargo except troops to the war zone in the Persian Gulf.

That required approximately 2500 qualified, licensed, officers and credentialed crewmen. The existing commercial fleet of U.S. flag ships had to produce those skilled civilian mariners, and the few remaining shipyards in this country had to provide the skilled workers to get those ships in seaworthy condition. At the time of this writing, there are no longer anywhere near enough active, credentialed merchant mariners to again pull off such a mobilization of ships to support our warriors as we managed for Desert Shield and Desert Storm.

So, what happened to all those ships in the U.S. Merchant Marine after Vietnam? Two major blows befell the ships and the shipyards that build and maintain them. Both were driven, as is so often the case in misfortune, by bold-faced greed.

The first blow came when American shipping companies rushed to get rid of their U.S. flag ships and operate ships registered in "Flag of Convenience" (FOC) countries like Panama, Liberia, the Bahamas, etc. This saved them vast sums in U.S. taxes as well as the costs of maintaining their ships to the standards required by the USCG for issuance Certificates of Inspection. They pay substandard wages to Third World crews who are regularly exploited in ways that ended for U.S. seamen with the Merchant Marine Acts of 1915 and 1920.

The second blow came as a classic example of unintended consequences. When the Oil Pollution Act of 1990 (OPA '90) was passed, it required all U.S. Flag tankers to be "double-hulled" by certain cut-off dates, based on the year they were built. Legislators envisioned that the existing fleet of U.S. tankers would simply be replaced by new, double-hull, ships. They did not understand that ship owners would instead replace these ships with tugboats and barges. That saved the owners a great deal of money in crew wages because USCG Regulations for tugs and barges require not only less crewmembers, but also officers with lower, limited, licenses. Those tugs and barges are not usable for military support overseas and those officers with limited, tugboat licenses are not qualified to man any of the ships in the reserve fleet to be called up for military service.

Adding to these circumstances, many Merchant Marine officers also have reserve Naval commissions. When they are called up to active Navy duty, the ranks available to man activated reserve cargo ships are further depleted, causing a dangerous shortage of qualified American civilian mariners in time of war.

The Merchant Marine Act of 1920 (The Jones Act) is the last remaining lifejacket that ensures there will be at least a minimal cadre of highly trained, qualified, and credentialed American merchant mariners to respond to the Oath of Allegiance that we all took to support our nation's military when called upon to do so in time of war or armed conflict. And without us, our armed conflicts cannot be supported overseas. They will instead be supported by truck drivers carrying munitions to the front lines here in the continental United States

The motto of the United States Merchant Marine is: "In Peace and War, 1775". That is worth a moment's reflection. Since the time of the American Revolution, we have needed a merchant marine during times of peace in order to ensure that we have them in times of war.

The Jones Act is federal law that remembers the hard-won lessons learned in our nation's armed conflicts for nearly 250 years. Honor it accordingly.

CHAPTER 3
Cruising: Cuba, Caribbean & More

In This Chapter
Sallee

In seafaring terms, cruise ships are ideal for some and an abomination in the views of others. The answer often lies within the means and condition of the traveler, and what they want from the sea.

Going to "sea" on a cruise ship is like saying you ran a marathon, when it was a "half-marathon" 13.1 miles, not 26.2 miles. But that is not to say running 13 miles isn't part of the experience. Just as "going to sea" in a huge hotel built for luxury, in smooth seas is a sea voyage. But it is hardly the same as the experience of a merchant marine seaman caught in a storm.

Cruise ships as a mode of sea travel has its pluses and barriers. Here we take you on all-inclusive cruises through the Caribbean, from Belize to old Cartagena, Aruba, up the Windward and Leeward Islands, to Puerto Rico. Capping the sea trip off, is Cuba. Then off to another cruise ship paradise, the Mediterranean, beginning in Rome.

Drop your bags with the Hawaiian-shirted International Longshoremen's Association bell hop, walk across the gangway and enter a wonderland of, casinos, Broadway-style shows, food and more food, all with spectacular service. No making your bed, doing laundry or packing, everyday a new port.

We meet the crew behind the scenes and learn how the USA leads in the passenger ocean ship race, with the SS *United States*. We peek at the future as the horn blasts and we go aboard.

And what happens at sea doesn't stay on the ship, it makes for good sea stories.

Even on large cruise ships one can experience solitude as the sun rises.

Cruise ships: Pluses & Minuses
Sallee

All Aboard!

The experience of cruising begins at the curb. Arriving at the cruise terminal is an experience. People pour out of cars, cabs and buses, all carrying far too much. Excitement is in the air and the bell caps, in colorful Hawaiian shirts, pile suitcases high on their carts, promising that every item will be delivered to your stateroom on board. Stuffing tips in their pockets they whisk your bags away.

You grab your carry-on bag, with your medicine, one change of clothes, and all of your documents. Entering the terminal building you present your papers, for the first of many times, to a part-time, often retired person, cruise line representative.

Meanwhile, behind the scenes on the wharf, two cruise ships are in port this morning, almost 8,000 people off and another 8,000 on with tons of luggage. All processed by International Longshoremen Association members.

Semi-trucks bumper to bumper pull up to loading docks. Forklifts dart in and out like humming birds to a flower, rushing meat, veggies, eggs, soda, and of course liquor aboard. Other forklifts dash in the other doorway with pallets of, you guessed it, tons of suitcases.

Now begins your Alice in Wonderland experience, trying to find your cabin. Off for lunch on the top deck and you begin to relax, realizing this trip is really happening. After checking your cabin a few more times to see if your bags have arrived, the muster station (abandon ship) drill begins.

Time to count 45 lifeboats and rafts, times 100, divided into 4,000 people. Okay, there are enough. Dismissed you are back on the lido deck, topside, you watch the ship slowly move from the wharf and begin your trip.

After 70 years of flying, I don't even notice takeoffs. On a ship, I notice. You roam around a 1,000- foot stage to find the best view. You wave and yell good-bye to those on the wharves. Hey, I can see my house from up here. The best view is seeing the *Elissa* slip past the stern as we head out. Who cares where we are going? I don't, my ship has left, this time with me.

Getting to Know You ... Sea Days

"So, are you going to write about me?" she said.

Staring out at the indigo deep blue sea, hands gripping the mahogany rail in a captain-like stance, I drift back to reality, if there is such a thing on a ship in the Caribbean. I look down to see Pat. Twinkling eyes behind large glasses. Her smile is framed by probably well-earned silver hair. Her husband Ed stands next to her, appearing thin, with black glasses and a goatee.

"Sure," I answered, wondering how they knew I wrote a newspaper column.

Had the *Galveston County Daily News* expanded to Williamson County, where they live? Maybe, after all, I hear from readers from all over. Pat explained she is a member of a writing club and shares she might like to read some interesting wharf stories. Each evening we sit at the same dinner table with eight other people, yet I don't remember mentioning the column.

We had stood at this same rail a week ago while leaving St. Maarten. They pointed out the Stars and Stripes boat sailed by Dennis Connors when he won the America's Cup. The couple excitedly recounted their adventure that afternoon blazing across the bay aboard the twelve-metre boat. These 70- something-year-olds were like kids recounting a visit to the Pleasure Pier. Now I remembered, I mentioned I had written a column about my sail boat race in Cozumel, promising I would email them a copy. Boy does Pat have a memory.

Another morning we had a leisurely sea day breakfast getting to know each other. This is a second marriage of twenty-five years for both of them. They met at a church singles event. Ed had a German Shepherd, she, three cats and four kids. While maybe it wasn't love at first sight, clearly something clicked, as they appear a very happy seasoned couple. Ed, an MIT graduate, worked for defense contractors on smart bombs.

They followed his job from Lewisville to Tucson and finally to Georgetown—Texas not D.C. As a nurse, Pat could find a job anywhere. In her last position, she traveled all over evaluating hospitals.

Sea days on the itinerary look boring, yet in reality, they can be as informative as a cultural tour on an island.

Cruising the Mediterranean

After a quick 12-hour flight from Houston to Rome, an hour taxi ride with Italian born friend Laura, and husband Robert, we end up in a Disneyland like scene in Rome. Up a 1920's style small cage elevator, I walked out and into our bedroom, threw open the shutters and gazed at a vista right out of a romantic movie. I began speaking with my hands.

A few days rushing through 2,000 years of history, including a drive down the Appian Way (Laura's cousin got lost), we headed up the coast to Civitavecchia, Rome's home seaport.

Across the gangway again aboard a cruise ship for a ten-day dash through the Med—Mediterranean, that is. One island after another, even in the same day. So fast. On a small bus, get off look at shops, jump in the sea for a swim in exquisite clear sapphire sea and back on board. Sicily, Malta, Blue Grottos, Santorini, Mykonos, Pompeii, blurred by.

The only day I fully remember was Athens, where we booked a private tour for just the six of us. Paul, the guide, knew Athens' ebb and how to avoid tourists. We had the Parthenon to ourselves, a friendly family style delicious Greek seafood lunch on a perfect curve beach. Hmm. The temple Poseidon overlooking the cobalt sea on three sides finished the far too short visit.

Pros and Cons of Cruise Ships:
Pros:
Inexpensive way to travel, all costs included.

No packing and unpacking every day. You wake up in a new location each morning.

No making the bed, cooking, or cleaning.

Easy trip to far-away places. Walk on, eat dinner, sleep and you are there.

Lots to do right out your cabin door, a walk on the deck in the sea air, lectures, games, movies, dances (if you can stay up that late) and Vegas-type shows.

Visit for hours with friends, new and old while looking out at the indigo sea.

Watch the blue ocean, moonlit night, or sunrise from your balcony.

No phones, meetings, deadlines—if you must, there are onboard computers and WiFi.

Quiet; time to think, read or write. Or take a nap.

Visit a different port and country almost every day.

Tour worry free, and all the guides speak your language.

Turn down service at the end of the day.

The name says it all: Freedom. In this case, it means go with the crowd.

Cons:

Pick the wrong ship or crew and you are stuck for seven days or more.

False advertising—Your "ocean view" is maybe an eight-inch dirty porthole.

Wait in stairwells, rush to the bus, rush to the sights, rush past views, blurred photos, rush back, stand in line to board. Too many ships in port at once.

No time for strolling or meeting the real people of a country. Drive by sightseeing.

Stuck traveling in another country with rude ugly Americans embarrassing you.

No feel of the sea through the huge ship's hull.

To Sum It All Up

Okay, the score is 12 for cruising, versus six for not cruising. Of course, one's options should be considered too. A multimillion dollar yacht with crew would flip the totals. Or a hop aboard sailboat as a crew member. Read *Ten Years Behind the Mast: The Voyage of Theodora R*, by Fritz Damler (Amazon). Fritz picked up crew members all over the world. They experienced 30-foot waves, days of calm and no air-conditioning. Plus, you had to travel light with no time restraints. Not an option or desire for most of us.

The threat of disease on a densely packed ship has always been a threat to the industry. Pandemic—COVID 19—cost the cruise lines and their ports of call millions of dollars. Already smaller—that is funny when the ships are 1,000 feet long—ships are being ordered to replace the new Oasis class monsters.

Cures for the cons are shots (vaccine, not whiskey) and *Cruise Critic*. The website lists details on almost every cabin on every ship, down to the square feet and nuance. Experienced cruisers can go with Trip Advisor self-guided tours. View short one day port visits as scouting trips to be returned to for extend stays. Down side, a long airplane ride. Then again, you could do a repositioning sea voyage.

What else does the future hold for this type of vacation? See Mike's predictions for the industry at the end of this chapter. Until then, cruise and relax on a sea day, then read on.

Nassau, My Kind of Port
Sallee

Nassau, my kind of town since 1974. My first cruise was three days out of Miami, the cost for two, $269. A conference add-on special. Destination: The Bahamas, James Bond-style, pre-development of Paradise Island.

Back then there was mainly the Straw Market, hundreds of years of history of pirates, colonial rule and slavery. Loyalists from America settled here beginning with the Revolutionary War. They brought their slaves with them.

I returned in 2010. Interesting story. I had retired the last day of 2009, and went to work the next day at the University of Houston-Downtown as a visiting professor. But Mother had heard only the word "retire" and made plans for me to take her, Aunt

Suzy and Uncle Wally on a Big Band-themed cruise out of Fort Lauderdale in February for 10 days.

My argument, was, "But Mother, I just took a new job, I can't ask the dean for a vacation right off." Having been an assistant dean herself, mother knew there were always ways around university rules. And she was right.

I was teaching online courses on child abuse, so I explained to the dean I would do research on how Caribbean countries were addressing the issue in their countries. Given I was teaching by computer, I would use the ship's Internet to check in each day with my students. I would do written "lectures" on what I found in each country. The dean liked the idea, replying, "Great idea, please copy me on your reports." Ha! No pressure. No need for the excursion booklet.

First stop, Nassau—named for the British Prince of Orange-Nassau—the capital and largest city, by far, of the 700 (yes, that is correct) something islands making up the Bahamas.

With no contacts in the Bahamas, I was first off the ship, after pleading with the tour director that I was on an important international assignment. The coat and tie helped. On Bay Street, I walked the cab line asking drivers if they knew where I could find the social services office.

Third cab down, the driver said, "Yes that would be the Department of Social Services." Perfect, off we went past the Queen's staircase, carved into the rock leading up to government offices, and the government house for parliament, around a few curves to a whitewashed concrete—probably hurricane proof—building. I asked the driver to wait for me.

"No problem, mon."

The receptionist caught on quickly that I was a professor from University of Houston wishing to meet the director. A few minutes later she returned, "Might I return at one o'clock?" I could meet with Mrs. Smith, the Assistant Director, and Dr. Jones, the chair of the Social Work program at the University of the Bahamas, who would be visiting.

Jackpot. "Yes, of course, I am honored," I answered.

On the way back to the ship I asked Jacob, the cab driver, if he could pick me up at 12:30 to take me back, and asked if he would be available to drive my mother around while I had my meeting.

"Of course "mon"."

I knew I wasn't in Jamaica; "mon" is the jargon of the Caribbean.

Back to the ship, back to the cabin. "Mother, do you want to have a tour of Nassau at noon?" I asked.

"Sure. I wasn't going to get off as I have been to Nassau so many times, but it will be good to drive by the sights."

Off to a wonderful time with Mrs. Smith and Dr. Jones. I was even asked if I would return and take the mail boat to many of the islands and teach Bahamas social workers what I had told Mrs. Smith.

"Well, I have to get back to U of H to teach, but maybe when I am really retired," was my answer. Over the years, I regretted not exploring a semester sabbatical, just to help Mrs. Smith, you understand.

Jacob picked me up. Mother had a trip down memory lane tour and was of course now best friends with Jacob. Cost: $100, even expensive for an excursion—but mother's happiness—priceless.

Dr. Jones did come to Houston to speak at one of our national conferences. Good trip, and the dean was very pleased with my reports. I also found out that one of my students had been born in the Bahamas.

Another one of my visits, in 2015, included another unexpected visit with an academic.

Next to the new Straw Market is a very special, powerful museum. I missed it on previous trips as it had two times been burned out. The Pompey Museum of Slavery and Emancipation, is officially named for the brave man who lead a slave revolt on another island, Exuma, in 1860, today a tourist spot. The museum is housed in the 1780 Vendue House, where slaves were sold.

This trip, recently retired for real, I was dressed as a tourist: Hawaiian shirt, shorts and sandals, topped off with a Panama straw hat. I approached the museum door. A bit early. Maybe a coffee and come back. Promptly at 9:00 a.m. the doors opened and the bright smiling face of a young woman, a descendant of slaves, greeted me.

"Would I sign their guest book?" she asked.

"Of course."

"Oh, you are a professor?"

"A retired professor."

"I am sure our director would like to meet you. She will be here at 9:30 a.m."

"But I am not dressed for meeting her."

"That is of no problem." This was a formal, "No problem, mon."

The museum, while small, impressively explains the message of "the experience of the enslaved throughout the ages," especially the "golden triangle" shipping of Africans to The Bahamas. A display of the last slave ship, the Peter Mowell, chronicles its wreck and the lives of the slaves who survived.

Right at 9:30, the director and a Harvard professor entered, Both of them professionally dressed Black administrators. I was formally introduced to a "t" and invited to join them upstairs in the board room. I politely tried to excuse myself, first on tourist dress, then lack of knowledge of the topic, but my words were gently hushed. We had a wonderful discussion, and they have a huge fan of their museum. Go see it! And donate more than the $3 admission fee.

On my most recent visit, after a day on Blue Lagoon Island, coming back on a boat tour of the harbor, I finally saw the house from *Thunderball*, my favorite Bond thriller. The Beach Boys version of the century old Bahamas folk song, the *Sloop John B* sound-soothed the soul and "around the Nassau town we did roam ..."

The Bahamas has it all.

Most Caribbean port towns have a statue or two. Here, author Sallee's brother-in-law, Dr. Douglas Bickerstaff, poses with a pirate on Cayman Island. (Doug is the one on the right.) Photo by Susan Bauer. Used with permission.

Behind the Scenes

Sallee

She spoke softly, with an accent, Tagalog, not easily understood by me. Middle-aged, her eyes had a hint of life's sadness.

His young eyes spoke of eagerness and excitement of being heard. I leaned forward, focused trying to understand, to appreciate; to learn the story of their lives.

Never seen by the 4,000 cruise ship passengers, Rosella and Javier work in the crew's mess. Almost 1,700 crew members live on board. Eating, sleeping and having clothes cleaned. I know something of their life from behind the scene tours.

Sometimes we don't want to see behind the curtain.

When our daughter, Joan, sang at Disneyland, the land of picture perfect fantasy, I was there front and center. Afterwards I went back behind stage with her. One of the biggest mistakes of my life. From age 5, all I had seen was perfection of the Magic Kingdom. Behind the fence was the ugly part of creating a fantasy. Garbage cans, rust, junk stacked up and Mickey smoking a cigarette.

Cruise ship passengers live in brilliant color, art and sculptures in massive staircases. The crew lives in institutional green and gray steel bulkheads. No dancers in feathers, tuxes or even fluffy towels. No faux marble, wall paper or beautifully set tables. Just linoleum top tables, no china or sparkling wine glasses.

Cabin stewards almost always speak perfect English with polished social skills—instant best friends to passengers; working for tips. Rosella and Javier work in the crew's dining area; no need for English and no tips.

Yet, this is a very well-paying job for them. From rural Philippines with few good jobs, salaries at sea are higher. Compensation comes with the price of absence from family and long hours of routine. The cost was in her eyes as she entered the Seafarers Center.

Rosella approached Outreach Coordinator Denise Hightower-Aguilar. She didn't even need to ask. "Yes, the bikes are reserved and ready to go."

They sat on the couch for a bit visiting, Rosella relaxed as the tension from her job eased. They planned their bike outing, down 23rd to the Seawall.

Off they went.

Two hours later, holding the door open Denise asked, "How was it?"

The answer was in Rosella's eyes. No translation needed.

Sitting on their favorite couch, sipping water, the duo, mother and adult son figures, listened to an improvised jam session of guitars, drums, keyboard and singing busboy. The instruments are available at the Center. The band were crew members. They are good musicians.

One waiter even sings during cruise ship dinners, Elvis style. Wonder if he gets paid scale?

The Center is an oasis, but if Rosella has day duty, she can't get off the ship.

Time is up. They select a few items from the counter. Denise bags them and discretely walks away, as Rosella and Javier make their donation to the jar. They smile, proud.

Then back to institutional green and gray.

For more sea stories visit a seafarers center in your home port.

Seafarer: Anastasia
Sallee

We began discussing which ships we really liked. She, from the perspective of a crew member, me as a passenger. We are at the Galveston Seafarers Center; a busy spot Anastasia visits every Sunday while her ship is in port.

"The ship I really liked was *Triumph*," I commented.

She said, "Well, it is in dry dock in Spain. When it is relaunched, it will be known as the *Sunrise*."

How nice I thought, I watched a number of sunrises over the Caribbean from its deck. (See the book *Galveston Wharf Stories*).

This late-twenties, blue eyed, light-blond haired, confident woman holds a critical position on the largest cruise ship in its fleet. She's in charge of inventory for all the items which are loaded each Sunday morning from the wharf into the ship. Everything from "Guys" hamburgers to pallets of beer, to pillow cases.

She has worked on cruise ships for five years, doing six-month contracts. At the end of each contract she can request a new ship. The catch is that given that there is only one position such as hers on each ship, she has few choices.

I ask how this life affects her friends and relationships.

She laughed. "My boyfriend has to follow me, as there are several waiters on each ship."

Her boyfriend is the headwaiter in the aft dining room starboard side. A few weeks ago, Maria, from Moscow had been our waitress. We asked to be at her table each evening, but given that we had "anytime dining", we never had her table again.

At the end of brunch, the last day I found her. We discussed Moscow, maneuvers in Russia and the new business model of huge cruise ships.

"I'm not sure if Maria would remember me." I told Anastasia, while hoping she would.

Anastasia's eyes lit up, "Oh yes, we know her. Maria's section was in my boyfriend's area," she said.

Within a couple of minutes, we realized we had a common friend.

We continue comparisons, moving on to things to do on each ship. She likes being on her current ship which boosts an IMAX Theater.

Anastasia looked forward to the end of this contract when she could return home for a few months. Her parents work in the banking industry and her 18-year-old sister is finishing school. For the past six months, Anastasia has only been able to talk to them once a week from here at the Center. She misses them but knows she is making much better money on the ship than in Belarus.

On the ship, she enjoys the small village of 1,500 crew members.

"You get to know everyone pretty soon."

Her cabin is nice but smaller than passenger cabins and she didn't get to choose it; the cabin is assigned to her position.

She asked if I had ever been to Belarus.

"No, the closest was Turkey. I really liked it before the dictator took over. I would not be welcomed by his people now."

"You should visit Egypt. It is very nice and safe."

All of a sudden, I was struck by the fact that English must be her second language, yet it was like speaking to a Midwesterner. And she'd make a great tour agent as well.

We discussed how the trains in Europe run at up to 310 km/h—192 miles per hour—and how healthcare there is free and taxes about the same as in the U.S.

"I guess we Americans believe we are the best in the world in everything, but of course we aren't."

She replied, "Certainly not when it comes to the Internet. You are way behind."

I thanked her for her time knowing she wanted to talk to her family. An amazing woman from a country most of us know nothing about. But she knows all about us.

A few weeks later in Starbucks, a woman, back turned to me, was texting away while waiting for her coffee. She looked familiar, but having just returned from a road trip to SoCal the night before I was a bit fuzzy. When she turned around, I realized it was Anastasia. She beamed that she just had two weeks to go on her contract.

Small world, at least on the Galveston wharf.

And it gives you a perspective on us.

The Seafarers Admiral: Mike Rodriguez
Sallee

It's a long way from Long Island, New York, to Galveston, Texas, yet for Rear Admiral Michael Rodriguez, it was even further. Seventeen years aboard merchant marine ships added many more miles with international experiences. A maritime labor official, staffer in U.S. Congress, Navy, and deputy administrator, Maritime Administration, led Rodriguez to be selected the superintendent of Texas A&M-Galveston's Maritime Academy.

He understands what cruise ship crews go through, away from home and family, so he also volunteers with the seafarers center. Among the many callings he held during his career, he always remembered the friendship he found in seafarers centers around the world.

"I remember when so many centers helped me when I was at sea. I am happy to work with the seafarers center now."

A seafarer's life is a challenge. With automation reducing crews down to 21 it is lonely. With three watches, there are only about seven people you see routinely. Even then as Rodriguez recalls, "You may only speak to someone over the phone from engine room to bridge on your watch and never actually meet them face to face."

Every sailor has sea tales and this admiral is no exception. In the old days, a pallet of movies on large metal reels in cans were delivered to the ship. One night was officer's night to control the projector the next night the crew's. This created interaction among the crew as they debated which films to see sometimes over and over. Movie night became a social event among the small group.

Technology arrives with social impacts. On merchant marine ships the VCR, which could be purchased inexpensively in foreign ports, allowed individuals to watch movies by themselves. Today, with personalized smartphones and individual cabins, social interaction on merchant ships has been reduced even further.

Rodriguez sees the need for the Seafarers Center playing an even greater role in the lives of seafarers. Even a trip to the local discount store is a welcome change of pace. Driving from the Port of Galveston through the historic homes provides a change in scenery, far different from the day-to-day view of the ocean. Visiting with the checkout clerk a cherished break from the monotonous sea days. Shore leave is a quality of life issue for seafarers.

Seafarers continue to face pressure from ship owners to reduce wages, healthcare and time ashore. Rodriguez recalls one case of where a Captain had to pay $800 for his family to catch a ride from the gate to the ship to spend a couple hours with him.

Thanks to regulations adopted by the U.S. Coast Guard, next year seafarers will have an easier time getting ashore without having to pay to see their family in a U.S. port.

"I am thrilled that seafarers can look forward to easy access to shore leave and loved ones. I worked with so many others on this issue. It has been a long time coming," he said.

And when in Galveston there may be an admiral at the wheel to drive seafarers to town.

Havana's Connection with Galveston
Sallee

Only two steps off the ship's gangway I passed back through centuries of colonialism, capitalism and communism. Welcome to Cuba.

"Albin? Albin?" Here is our guide, Lou, and the driver, Julio, of our sort-of 1956 Cadillac. As the grandson of Chevrolet Charlie, I know every year and model of 1950-1968 American made cars. This is fantastic.

Lou was excited. Wearing a 1940's style straw hat and shorts he shouted: "You're from Galveston? In the 1920s my grandfather used to go fishing for 10 days out of Havana. Where he really went was to Galveston with a boat load of rum during Prohibition."

I explained that was part of our history and the makings of a famous family, barber brothers turned entertainment masters, the Maceos. Their story was even made into a play. A relative, Tilman Fertitta, created a multibillion-dollar company, including the Houston Rockets. "Wow, maybe we should've stayed in touch with them?" Lou responded.

I am not sure that would've done much good as many Cubans have not been allowed to travel outside their country during their whole lives. Thus, the Cuban rafts we have found in the Gulf.

Lou is a rare exception. As an economist, he worked for the government traveling to many countries negotiating contracts for Cuba.

As we toured the Castillo, I asked if he had ever seen the forts in Cartagena. "Oh yes," he said, and he'd been to Quito, Río de Janeiro and about five other major South American cities my ears could not keep up with. He knew his stuff. His stories rang true to me. Of course, I have only two trips to Colombia to go by.

As we headed off to Ernest Hemingway's home, Lou explained the demographics of Cuba. Considered a white Spanish gentleman, he said 60 percent of the country in 1960 was white, now down to about 37 percent. The largest group is a blend of Spanish and African referred to as "mulatto", a term not always accepted in good company in the USA. Eleven percent are black.

The literacy rate among the 11 million Cubanos is 99 percent as reported by the CIA. Universal education.

Julio, our driver, has never been off the island. He'd like to visit new places. Manuel, another driver, is an Italian who chooses to live in Cuba. With his dark hair pulled back into a tight ponytail, mouth always with a smile, he's a hunk. While he travels routinely back to Italy he feels more comfortable in Havana than Rome.

Certainly, there is far less traffic here. Driving four days a week he is able to afford a comfortable high-rise apartment facing the sea.

In Hemingway's home, or should we say Martha Gellhorn's, bright white walled rooms are minimally decorated with symbols of his life. Each room is roped off. As I began shooting photos through the doorway of his office, an attractive uniformed docent quietly approached. "Would you like me to take some pictures?"

Slipping her my camera, I said, "Gracias." Expertly framing each shot, she returned within a minute.

"Do you have a little something for me?" she asked.

I shook her hand with a $3 Cuban bill. Her eyes spoke. The photos were certainly worth the money, not to mention the seductive smile.

Back on the road Lou shared that he had two sons, both college-educated, an architect and a sports trainer. Neither can leave. They work for the government at about $20 a month plus free health care. Lou has big dreams for them.

We visited about families intermittently as we cruised through neighborhoods and alleyways accented with wires and poles, Galveston style. Otherwise the landscape was assessed through diesel haze of gray. Every mile or so a patch of green, a community park, a gathering place.

At these verde junctures Cubano eyes came alive, resiliency shone from the soul, insight decorated each statement, drowning out even a U.S. professor's knowledge of the past. The present is dismissed by "we have survived worse."

Right now, we are all amigos in historical Havana.

Passenger Ships & Cruise Ships
Leahy

The greatest of the American passenger ships, the *SS United States*, had her keel laid for United States Lines in 1952, the year I was born. Two others, somewhat smaller but of similar luxury, the *SS Independence* and the *SS Constitution*, began construction for American Export Lines the two previous years. It was still the time when vessels that seamen call passenger ships were referred to as ocean liners for marketing to the transatlantic traveling public. Today the term cruise ship is used for the same purpose.

Photo of the SS United States donated to the SS United States Conservancy by Nick Landiak.

The days when shipping companies made the bulk of their income on passenger ships from Europeans immigrating to America had already passed by then, as the great waves of late 19th and early 20th Century immigration had slowed to a trickle and for some time the main source of income on these ships had been travelers between America and Europe who expected to have a distinctly luxurious experience during the crossing. Marketing by American and European shipping companies emphasized that half the wonders of a trip to London, Paris, or Rome was in the voyage across the sea.

The United States was by no means alone, the great

shipping lines of France, Holland, Italy, and the United Kingdom boasted many beautiful ocean liners. These vessels had all been called into service as troop ships and hospital ships during the recent WWII, some with tragic ends like France's magnificent *Normandie*. With that national defense lesson learned, the new ocean liners being built at the end of the 1940's and early 1950's were typically subsidized by their home countries' governments to ensure their availability in time of war. Our governments, like the great steamship lines, did not yet realize what the post war advances in aircraft would do.

The *Independence*, the *Constitution* and the American flagship that seamen still refer to as the "Big U" (*SS United States*) were barely in service for a decade before the term "Jet Set" began appearing in newspapers, magazines, and television. The wealthy industrialists, Hollywood celebrities, famous athletes, and idle European ex-royalty that were by then the lifeblood of the ocean liners discovered they could cross the Atlantic in just a matter of hours instead of days, and if the first-class accommodations of a jetliner were to a lesser standard than on an ocean liner, well, it was just for a few hours. Being part of the "Jet Set" began to win them more media attention since the once plentiful newspaper photographers had stopped haunting the west side piers of New York.

For some time, the end of the era of the great ocean liners was thought to be the end of passenger ships. But a new business model eventually developed. These are the vessels today called cruise ships whose purpose is to simply take passengers in varying degrees of luxury on trips to beautiful places and back again. American owned companies, notably Carnival Cruise Lines, discovered they could build ever-larger ships, resembling floating versions of the high-rise rectangles of the condominiums that now line the beach front of places like Galveston and Miami.

I think the next era, will show a substantial increase in people more interested in sailing in much smaller vessels that represent less possible risk of pandemics to their health. The behemoth ships, so costly to build and maintain, will pass from favor of the sailing (cruising) public and find their way to the breaker yards of India, Turkey, Pakistan, and Taiwan.

The future will lie in much smaller vessels like those now sailing the rivers of Europe, the islands of the Caribbean, and the waters of Alaska and the Antarctic. These smaller, specialty cruise vessels now represent only a small fraction of the annual number of people taking cruise vacations, but I think that will change.

The days of ocean liners serving the needs of vast numbers of poor immigrants to cross the ocean, and the days of wealthy celebrities enjoying the luxurious life of a world-class ocean passage have all passed. Similarly, the days of vast numbers of the middle class enjoying moderately luxurious cruises with a destination that is only to return to the original port of embarkation may well be passing now. The business model of small vessels sailing in unique waters and corners of the world, may now find itself on the ascendancy when a pandemic threat passes astern. For more on SS *United States* visit: *www.ssusc.com*

SS United States today waiting for rescue in Philadelphia.
Photo taken from drone by Chuck Homler.

CHAPTER 4
Nature's Strength on the Seas

Red sky at night, sailor's delight. Sunset over Clear Lake taken from the sailboat Capt. Kidd. (Photo by Capt. Joe Stumpf. Used with permission.)

In This Chapter
Sallee

Red sky at night, sailor's delight.

Red sky at morning, sailors take warning.

This rhyme is one heard around mariners everywhere, for well over 2,000 years. The saying is even cited in Matthew 16:2-3 in the New Testament as established wisdom that prevailed among the Jews of the Second Temple Period. (Wikipedia)

The Revised Standard Version of the Bible states: When it is evening, you say, "It will be fair weather; for the sky is red." And in the morning, "It will be stormy today, for the sky is red and threatening." You know how to interpret the appearance of the sky, but you cannot interpret the signs of the times.

We need to accept the translation of the Revised Standard Version, as when I took New Testament Greek in college, I translated only John. I would have preferred Matthew. Now we know why. And in my career as a professor, my use of Greek was mainly to differentiate between names of fraternities and sororities.

Before seafarers adopted the saying, it was probably used by shepherds. Still the theme is true. If in the morning, particulates in the air get kicked up it usually forwards rough weather.

We know that from rust, to fog, to hurricanes, nature plays a critical role in any human activity on the high seas. From the first voyages in small sailing vessels to today's mega tankers, foul meteorological conditions always challenge those who do not take the environment seriously.

In this chapter, we present rough sea stories, from a sailing adventure on Galveston Bay and surviving hurricanes, to the progression of the sinking of a ship and loss of 33 U.S. men and women. A qualified seafarer respects and understands the natural elements when going down to the sea.

Mad Dogs & Englishmen
Sallee

First *Ann*, then *Joanna* passed us—exciting. I was sitting in a small 30-foot sailboat in the Houston Ship Channel when *Joanna's* —a container ship, 1,105-feet long, 150-foot beam—wake created an 8-foot wave which plowed our sailboat's bow into the sea. I think the right word is exciting. For some people, it might be scary. For the four of us this was bay sailing at its best.

I had emailed Capt. Mike Janota about Schooner Sunday at the Sea Star Base. He replied the racing boat needed to be ferried back from the Houston Yacht Club.

So, in the cold spring morning we began to rig *Lift Off*, me pushing sails up through the hatch while Capt. Matt Coulson, Mike Camm, and Dick Gray completed the technical tasks necessary to set the sails. Within minutes we were ready to cast off lines. Stepping onto the dock to untie the lines, I wondered how I was going to get back on, as there was a strong wind blowing the boat out into open water. These experienced sailors knew the trick. They pulled the boat up against the dock, I stepped over the safety cable, they released the line and off we went.

We shot out in the choppy north Galveston Bay with a 20-knot wind pushing us not always where we wanted to go. No other sailboats visible, only Mad Dogs and Englishmen, in our case Mike from the United Kingdom.

After two gybes, one where I got my shoulder blocked while ducking (sailors know what that is—stupid and painful—a large, high-speed bar of aluminum missed my head, but smacked my shoulder, not the good one), we were in the Houston channel. Which was a good thing. Most of Galveston Bay is very shallow and we had a keel.

The deep channel is where we needed to be, until *Ann* and *Joanna* came by. Then we surfed the waves 10 knots—fast. You had better hang on to something solid.

Sailboat Capt. Kidd hitting two-foot rough seas in Galveston Bay, similar to Lift Off's experience. Just add eight foot wakes from cargo ships. (Used with permission of Capt. Joe Stumpf.)

Behind the Texas City Dike the wind dropped and the sea smoothed out. Dick asked, "Alvin, want to take a turn?"

My first time on a tiller. It's confusing. The direction you pull the tiller is the opposite way the boat goes.

Running straight, staying to the right up the shallow channel, as per Capt. Matt's instructions, I was closely listening to Dick's story about how his dad's beautiful wood sloop almost ran aground.

Lift Off quickly but smoothly slammed on its brakes. Actually, the keel went into the sand 5-feet below us. Not to worry, the sail was tightened, the tiller pulled over and in less than a minute, which seemed like an hour to me, we slid back into the channel.

"That's strange. You were right on the edge, but the tide is low," Dick commented.

We glided under Interstate 45. No traffic jam down here, just another memorable day on the bay.

If you would like an enjoyable sailing experience or a wild ride, visit www.ssbgalveston.org. Another Galveston treasure.

El Faro, Crooked Island & a Hurricane
Sallee

El Faro has been on my mind since hearing of its sinking during Hurricane Joaquin in October 2015 off Crooked Island, the Bahamas. *El Faro,* an 800-foot cargo ship was just like the ones motoring down the Houston channel every day. All 33 U.S. crew were lost at sea. Sad, but soon forgotten.

Except this time. Crooked Island rang a bell. It is the winter home of Fritz Damler and Mari Anderson. Their wonderful book, *Plunge: Midlife with Snorkel* (Amazon), details building their beachfront home.

Shortly after Joaquin, eating lunch with Mari and Fritz in New Mexico, I carefully raised the question regarding hurricane damage.

Fritz summed it up. "All low-lying areas of the Island were inundated with up to eight feet of saltwater—roads and utilities wiped out. Homes were flooded, destroying appliances and vehicles. Our home fared pretty well with mostly wind damage to roofing and windows. The garage roof flew a quarter-mile down the beach and augured into a sandy bluff but the contents of said garage were spared. Fortunately, there was no loss of life. We're heading down in January to make repairs."

As only a landlubber and cruise ship rider, I was not familiar with Crooked Island. It sounded exotic and way off the beaten, or sailed, path.

Come to find out, just 35 miles off-shore is a busy shipping route, Florida to the Eastern Caribbean. This is the course Capt. Michael Davidson chose trying to miss the predicted northern path of Joaquin. As Galvestonians know, hurricanes have minds of their own, as Joaquin did, heading south before hooking north.

Waves rose to mountains. CBS's *60 Minutes* reported engine power was lost, probably causing the ship to broach, turning sideways to the waves. Without propulsion, the ship was at the mercy of the sea. The top two decks of the aft "skyscraper" were torn off, including the bridge with the captain.

When you visit a port, see how high up on a container ship the bridge is located. The waves' size and supremacy are difficult to imagine.

Now look at the stern of the ship and you probably will see a fully enclosed orange lifeboat on the ship. The 40-year-old *El Faro* was grand-parented in—open lifeboats were allowed. One boat was found, empty. Not a fair fight trying to survive in 140 mph-wind-whipped seas.

El Faro now sets upright 15,000 feet deep off Crooked Island—deeper than *Titanic*. The orange "black box," which would answer many questions, has not been located to date. (It was later found—see Mike Leahy's story after this one.)

What did the husbands, new dads, brothers, daughters, and sons face before their deaths? What was the rush to get to Puerto Rico? Why the risk, sailing into a hurricane? We don't know for sure, yet. One relative concluded the answer was to get frozen chicken there fast. Greed?

What a high cost. Thirty-three American seafarers lost off Crooked Island. CNN reported that using an old law, the ship owners have already sued to limit possible claims of the families. What future will their children, siblings and parents experience without them?

Victims of more greed?

SS El Faro. Photo by Tote Maritime.

What Happened: SS El Faro

Author Mike Leahy, who is familiar with the SS El Faro, having conducted a survey of the vessel for modifications in the 1990s, offers the following comments:

Having listened multiple times to the transcript of the Voyage Data Recorder (VDR) after it was released, it is clear that the initial information provided to the news media was not based on facts. The clear implication was that loss of the ship's propulsion caused the casualty and ultimate foundering of the ship. This was a case of putting the "cart before the horse".

It is my belief that the VDR audio transcript clearly shows the root cause of the casualty to be ever-increasing seawater ingress into the cargo hold from an unsecured scuttle (manway hatch into the hold). This belief is consistent with the findings in the NTSB and USCG final reports, as well. The 15 degrees of list reported by the captain early on is itself extreme, and, as water enters the hold, it flows inevitably to the listed side, so the list could only continue to increase.

It should be understood that steam powered main engines cannot operate with a list this severe because the lube oil in the main engine sump also inevitably flows to the listed side. This will cause the main lube oil pump to lose suction and discharge pressure and the hydraulic trip will slam the steam throttle valve to the engine shut in order to save the main engine bearings and main reduction gears. This trip feature exists to prevent a catastrophic failure of the main engine bearings and reduction gears, which would occur within minutes without lube oil to them. The engineers and engine crew would have been struggling to the very end in an effort to overcome this impossible handicap.

The root cause of the casualty and foundering, as revealed by the VDR transcript, would appear to be the failure of watertight integrity of the cargo hold, leading to sea ingress, severe and increasing list, and consequentially to the loss of operability of the main engine. Not the other way around.

Also, a note regarding this ship's open-style lifeboats, which were standard on thousands of ships for decades of ocean service prior to the development of enclosed lifeboats on newer ships. It is certainly true that the survivability of persons in an open lifeboat during a hurricane is significantly less than an enclosed lifeboat, but in the case of the *El Faro*, this must be seen as a tragically moot point.

Lifeboats and the davits from which they are suspended are deployed by gravity (so they can be deployed when abandoning a ship that has lost power). With a list of 15 degrees or greater in such a storm it is unlikely that the lifeboats on either side of the ship, whether they were of open or enclosed design, would be capable of being deployed.

Further, the record of the VDR transcript clearly shows the captain calling the chief engineer down below and telling him to ignore the abandon ship signal (given by the captain using the ship's whistle and general alarm bell) because he was only sounding it to assemble the rest of the crew. It is reasonable to presume by that call that he knew the boats could not be lowered and did not intend to risk lives by trying. Just a few minutes later the VDR transcript stops, indicating the wheelhouse had begun to suffer ingress from the sea.

When the vessel was located and videoed on the seafloor, it was noted that the entire bridge deck had separated from the rest of the superstructure as a unit (which is how it was originally fabricated). It is unlikely that this clean break could have been caused by the sea on the surface. Far more likely is that this separation occurred due to the tremendous pressure forces to which the ship's structure would have been subjected as she sunk to the great depth at which she now rests.

In summary, the ship's voyage plan, routed between the hurricane and the islands rather than following the Florida coast and keeping the islands between the hurricane and the ship, was an unnecessarily risky one and the sea, as is its wont, found the vessel's single point vulnerability: an unsecured cargo hold opening. Each moment of the resulting catastrophe followed like links of chain.

The final photograph taken of the El Faro by TMPR Terminal Manager on September 29, 2015, showing starboard list of approximately 4 degrees during loading operations prior to the final voyage. Credit: U.S. Coast Guard.

Hurricane Juan

Leahy

Hurricane Juan blew up with little warning in the Gulf of Mexico in the fall of 1985. Unlike storms that track across the Atlantic and Caribbean before entering the Gulf, those that develop right in the Gulf itself provide short notice to folks ashore and those at sea as well. Several people lost their lives in Juan on vessels and on offshore oil rigs, of which there are hundreds out in the Gulf of Mexico. Rigs likely to be in harm's way are normally evacuated for tropical storms and hurricanes, but with a short-notice storm like Juan, this is difficult to accomplish.

I encountered Juan while I was onboard a 72,000-deadweight-ton oil tanker, fully loaded with North Slope crude oil (from the Alaska oilfield), which we were carrying from Chiriquí Grande, Panama, and intending to discharge in St. James, Louisiana, upriver from New Orleans. The figure of 72,000 tons is an indication of how much crude oil cargo was onboard.

She was approximately 700 feet long by 100 feet wide and 25,000 shaft horsepower. The "split house" design is unique, and it is helpful to understand it when considering her operation in a serious storm. There is a catwalk running longitudinally from the aft house to the midship house approximately 10-12 feet above the aft well deck so crew members can pass safely, in particular while at sea. In large enough seas, like those in a hurricane, the fo'c'sle and even the catwalk can be washed over by the sea, making a crew member's run from one end to the other between waves a risky dash.

So, on this fall morning, as our ship diverted course so as to avoid the worst of Hurricane Juan, we were taking seas over the fo'c'sle itself, the well deck both fore and aft of the midship house was awash and so was the catwalk. Indeed, seas running over the length of the ship were breaking against the steel forward bulkhead of aft house some 30-40 feet above the waterline and even occasionally splashing down through the engine room skylights one deck higher yet, and draining down onto the hot steam pipes and turbines below, flashing to steam on contact and leaving the smell of burning salt throughout the machinery spaces.

It was a real seaman's day out in the normally quiet Gulf. I was 2nd engineer on this ship and it was shortly after I assumed the engine room watch at 0400 that morning that the mate called down from the bridge on the sound-powered phone used for voice communications between key locations on the ship. He asked me to slow the ship down from full sea speed to full ahead maneuvering speed, which is a reduction of about 20-30 shaft RPM, but also involves making several changes to the auxiliary steam machinery and reducing the firing rate in the boilers.

With the retrofitted automation on the boilers' combustion control and burner management systems, which were installed to eliminate the fireman-water tender's jobs, this modification to the way the boilers were being fired was supposed to happen automatically but it was untrustworthy. At a time when it was absolutely critical to ensure that propulsion power was not lost, even briefly, it was just prudent to make manual changes to the boiler controls.

Losing a steam plant for any reason does not involve just putting her in neutral and turning the key like an automobile. It can take several hours of work in brutally hot and physically unstable conditions by the engineers and black gang, while the massive ship is without steerageway and therefore at the mercy of the sea. This outcome must be prevented at all costs. If the ship begins to roll severely it can cause the level of the lube oil in the main engine sump to fluctuate to excess, which in turn will cause the main steam throttle valve to trip closed and in these conditions, it can be very difficult if not impossible to reset it and regain propulsion and steerageway.

Some 30 years later, in 2016, the consequences of this kind of situation were tragically demonstrated. When cargo holds on the *SS El Faro* began flooding with seawater coming in through an unsecured deck scuttle, the ship took a list so severe that it forced exactly this situation. The list on the *El Faro* caused the lube oil sump to run low on one side; the lube oil pump lost suction and the resulting lack of lube oil pressure tripped out the steam throttle valve to the main engine. Despite Herculean efforts, the engineers and black gang could not get it restored with the extreme and ever-increasing list. The outcome was that the *El Faro*, and her full complement of officers and crew, were lost in Hurricane Joaquin.

As dawn broke that morning, the 2nd mate went out on the deck on the aft side of the midship house and took a photo of a typical sea just beginning to wash over the well deck and catwalk and crash against the aft superstructure of the ship. It is such a striking photo that it was used in the next year's calendar from the American Maritime Officers. In it the black smoke coming from the boiler stack can be seen making a 90 degree turn to the horizontal, a result of the powerful winds.

I was on watch below when that photo was taken and have been asked why the smoke was so black; normally the most fuel-efficient combustion mixture results in a grayish brown haze called "economy haze". But on that day, I manually adjusted the fuel to air ratio to heavy on the oil because I was a lot more interested in ensuring we did not lose a fire in the boilers, no matter how briefly, than whether I was burning a little too much bunkers!

Forty-foot-high seas wash over the entire twenty-foot above the water line well deck of Mike Leahy's tanker during Hurricane Juan in the Gulf of Mexico. Photo courtesy of Leahy.

During my evening watch from 1600-2000, the captain called down from the bridge to advise me that we had received a call from the Coast Guard, relaying a mayday call from two men on a small sailboat. They had been forced to abandon all attempts to navigate their boat and battened down the boat with all the watertight openings secured and reported to the Coast Guard that they had twice been completely rolled over 360 degrees.

We were the nearest ship to their position and the captain was letting me know that he anticipated giving me bells in order to maneuver the ship into the best position and try to take the two men onboard our ship. Giving bells means that he would have the mate on watch ring various speed and direction orders on the engine order telegraph (EOT).

Ringing down orders like half ahead, slow ahead, dead slow astern, etc. is normal operations when a ship is in maneuvering waters coming into or leaving a port, docking the vessel, etc., but this normally never occurs at sea. It was for this reason he was giving me warning to prevent surprise and to ensure that I was standing by at the throttles and not away making an inspection round throughout the machinery spaces.

What followed was one of the finest examples of ship handling, seamanship, and basic courage on the part of our captain, chief mate and deck gang. The captain took the conn on the bridge and kept with him the 3rd mate to relay his engine orders on the telegraph, one able bodied seaman (AB) to serve as quartermaster and steer the ship, and one ordinary seaman to assist him as a messenger.

The task ahead was volunteer only and every last man jack volunteered. The captain maneuvered that massive 72,000 tons of steel and crude oil right down onto that little sailboat from upwind, creating protection from the brutal wind on the leeward side of our ship. But both our ship and the little sailboat were rising and falling approximately 40 feet vertically with each wave, and waves were periodically crashing across the well deck despite the captain's best effort to maneuver the ship to mitigate it. This put the rescue team in danger of being washed overboard or injured on the deck.

The engine room of a ship of this design is a very special place. The heat and the noise in this world of steam machinery is something that comes as a shock to those entering it for the first time. The coolest places (directly below a ventilation blower) are still well above 100 degrees Fahrenheit and in the hot corners above the boilers it is more like 130 degrees. Those in the engine and fire rooms always stay completely soaked with sweat and the air from the ventilator outlet blowing across our wet cotton boiler suits provides cooling.

When first entering an especially hot engine room it is sometimes necessary to dump a pot of water over our heads to soak our boiler suits, rather than waiting for sweat to soak us through. Most engine room crew also wear bandanas or Landry caps to keep the sweat out of our eyes. There are dispensers of salt tablets permanently mounted at key locations in the machinery spaces to replenish the salt lost by sweating and prevent a man from cramping or passing out.

Shortly after the captain called to warn me that he would soon be giving me maneuvering bells, the chief engineer came down from his office to standby in case a problem developed, and I needed assistance. I realized they were about to start the effort to transfer the men from the sailboat to our ship and needed the 30-ton propeller to stop turning in case some unfortunate soul ended up in the water.

Down in the engine room, this is all I knew about what was happening up on deck until it was over and the captain called down to tell me to bring the ship slowly back up to full speed ahead as he brought her back to her original course and let me know the rescue had been a success.

As the ship came down on the sailboat blocking the wind, the rescue team went out onto the port side of well deck aft of the midship house and passed body harnesses down to the two men on the boat. With gantlines attached to the harnesses, two AB's took the gantlines to nearby mooring bitts so that they could control them to prevent any slack as the men transferred. This way, the ship and the boat continued to rise and fall together vertically with each 40ft. wave.

The mate told me later that the fear he could see in eyes of those two men as the sailboat rose on the wave and they prepared to jump was like nothing he had ever seen before and he doubted he would see again. But they overcame their fear and jumped.

There is a long, even ancient history of seafarers risking their own lives in order to save fellow mariners in distress. For a seaman, there is no greater sense of fulfillment than when he has the opportunity to participate in such an event. That ship had one of the very best crews, from top to bottom, with whom I have ever had the honor to sail.

Footnote: At lunch the next day in the officer's saloon, these rescued sailors told us that they had been out taking someone else's new sailboat on a sea trial and that there was no insurance on the boat. They seemed extraordinarily distressed that we had not also saved their boat, although they must surely have realized that would have been impossible under the conditions. This story sounded a little less than plausible but, maybe it was true.

I do know that pleasure boats, sail and motor, coming up to small Gulf Coast ports carrying "special" cargos from Central and South America are not an uncommon thing. The spirit of gratitude also seemed to fade rather fast when they realized the ship would not be diverting to return them. Upon docking, they disappeared down the gangway the moment it was set in place. Never seen or heard from again.

Tanker on a typical day at sea in the Gulf of Alaska. Photo courtesy of Leahy.

Ghost Ships
Sallee

Something didn't feel right. I was in our cabin on the *Triumph* cruise ship approaching the Yucatan Strait. We were north of Cozumel by a day's cruising at 22 knots, so about 650 miles.

The ship began a wide U-turn, and then began to slow. While this was before the *Triumph* had its problems, I was still concerned. The ship's captain announced that he had seen a small boat adrift and by the laws of the sea, we were required to provide assistance.

Out on the balcony, I looked down. About 60 feet directly below was a 14-foot run-about boat. There were flip-flops on the seat next to a cell phone. The overhead canvas was torn a bit. No one to be seen. Were they diving? No, I thought. It is 12,000 feet deep here.

Finding no one, we continued on our way while the captain explained that the boat had become untied in Tampa and drifted to the far western stretch of the Gulf of Mexico, a distance of about 500 miles. The Mexican Navy would remove the boat as a hazard. Okay, nice try, but there had to be more to this ghost boat story.

My experience was just a small peek into the problem. Ghost ships have been around for hundreds of years, floating without a crew. Today, however most ghost ships have crews.

According to *The Guardian*, there has been a dramatic rise in cases of ghost ships. From 2004 through 2018 worldwide, 4,866 seafarers on a total of 336 vessels have been recorded as abandoned on board ship.

Human rights groups have compared abandonment to forced labor, or modern-day slavery. If a crew member leaves the ghost ship they forfeit their pay. For a captain, this might be $4,000 per month.

The Guardian goes on, "The majority of abandonment cases last between five and eight months, according to the International Maritime Organization. But, in some jurisdictions, lax laws allow unscrupulous ship owners to leave seafarers abandoned without pay, fuel and supplies, for longer. Seafarers rights groups are lobbying for the same human rights law governing land to apply at sea."

Seafarers often survive on only a rice diet and donations from onshore Seafarer Centers.

And then there are real ghost ships such as the MV *Alta*, which, after the crew was rescued off of the Bahamas by the U.S. Coast Guard, traversed the Atlantic crewless for more than a year. The 77-meter-long ship finally came ashore on the rocks in County Cork, Ireland. Fortunately, it didn't break up and spill oil on the sand. A survey crew did the damage assessment and plan for the ship's removal. The kind of work that Mike Leahy does.

Alta had floated over to Africa, up past Spain, then on to the Irish coast, just one of the increasing ghost ships on the high seas.

Note: At press time, the Alta was still not salvaged as it lies beached broadside to the sea continuing to be pounded by the waves. The city council tried to find funds to unload the remaining fuel on board. Having gone through numerous owners, none taking responsibility, the ship is abandoned. This ghost ship is truly a horror to the people of Ireland.

Fog engulfs the trolley stop by the Galveston Wharves. Coastal fog creates costly challenges to shipping several times a year.

Fog: Nature's Stop Sign
Sallee

Driving down Harborside Drive, only two soft red glows of taillights could occasionally be seen in the gray, dripping dense fog. Turning right onto 25th I find a parking space, I think—it is difficult to see the high grey curb (the British spelling of gray, as I parked on the Strand, another term borrowed from the English).

Up to the eighth floor, I am ushered back to the Director of Port Operations, Brett Milutin. His office window looks out at what was a grand panoramic scene of the harbor, but this morning's view was just water on the window, Navy gray. We get down to business, fighting the gray enemy: fog.

During fog attacks, the Galveston Bay Port Coordination Team (PCT) meetings are held each morning at 9 a.m. with all 70 interested parties. The PCT includes the U.S. Coast Guard, tug boat, oil, shipping, and fueling companies plus ship's agents and security agencies. Milutin is the chair.

The theme of fog along wharves is found in the lives of pilots, port operations, cruise ship headquarters, hotels, 18-wheelers, buses and ship's agents. It is a force of nature which can bring movement on the sea to a slow stop which requires coordination to avoid titanic tragedies.

There are numerous examples of ship captains trying to make a fast turn-around and pilots disagreeing. Inbound one morning a Galveston pilot had to hold his ground by stopping the ship against the captain's protest, waiting until the fog lifted. As the fog slipped away two kayakers were spotted just clearing the channel.

A close call for them and the kayakers probably didn't even know it.

One critical player in management of the sea, most of us landlubbers don't know about, is the MARAD, the Maritime Administration. This government agency is charged with keeping a strong merchant marine including being able to support our military deployments. Not something we want to do in a fog.

Members of the PCT prioritize which vessels will come and go when the fog lifts. Cruise ships and produce vessels are usually at the top of the list. Until then, ships remain tied to the wharf or find anchorage offshore.

During the meetings pilots have a great deal of influence. They have the experience to know what sight limits are necessary along the channels which vessels must take from the sea buoy to the wharves.

One Saturday a friend from Houston, Maureen, called while I was out of state and asked if she could stay in our spare apartment that night.

She explained that the fog had come in so thick she could not drive back to Houston. There were no rooms available in town. Two cruise ships were stuck off-shore and all the folks who were leaving that day had no place to stay. What a mess, and this is just one day and two ships.

Fog helped close the beautiful new Houston cruise ship terminal in Baytown for good. After only two years the two cruise lines using the $100-million-dollar facility cancelled their contracts due to fog-related costs. Steaming two hours up a narrow channel across the Bay cost enough, but adding additional fog related expenses was too much. Unlike the Port of Galveston there are no hotels or restaurants by the Houston Port, just container wharves. The fog won.

Fog brings a mysterious feel to events, such as the story about the old San Juan, Puerto Rico, guard who disappeared in the night fog. Or war ships, from Civil War sailing schooners to German U-boats during the Second World War, moving in and out of the fog off the coast.

What is this stuff called fog? It's a thick cloud of tiny water droplets suspended in the atmosphere near the earth's surface, according to one source. Sort of takes the romance out of the feeling one gets standing aboard a ship, gray everywhere, fog horn sounding in the distance.

Of course, there is always the concept of one's mind being in a fog. This state has come over me a number of times while settling into the routine aboard a cruise ship. Is this a sea day or will we dock, and if so where? I wonder. Along the coast fog is often present, whether in the air or in my mind.

The fog is lifting now as I finish this piece. Ship's agents, pilots and captains are glad to go back to full speed ahead. And Brett has his harborside view back.

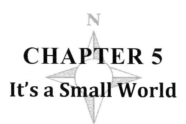

CHAPTER 5
It's a Small World

In this Chapter
Sallee

It's a small world after all!

We know this Disneyland song from the 1964 *New York World's Fair*, where I first rode a small boat through the flat cutouts depicting cultures from around the globe. The tune tends to stick in your mind all day. But then again that was the brilliance of Walt Disney.

And it's true, it really is a small world after all. Traveling through the world as both Mike and I have, it is such a surprise to find someone somewhere you'd never expect to see them, or to see someone you thought you'd never meet again.

From unexpected relatives, as Mike found after a hospital stay in Panama, to my experience on a Caribbean island bumping (literally) into a pirate captain I knew, we have bundles of stories describing such encounters.

Two components are found in these chance meetings. First is the fact that the other person is even in the same port or on the same island at the same time. And the second, mind-boggling element, is actually being in the *exact* same place at the *exact* same time. How often have you made careful plans to meet someone somewhere and they are not there? Right.

Follow us along in this chapter as we stumble upon people in unexpected places, from Ciudad Panama to Singapore and throughout the Caribbean. Keep your eyes up and your ears open for former sights, sounds and persons we know. Here we go.

It's a small world after all ...

Jewel noses up to a gate on the Panama Canal,
one of the busiest shipping spots on the sea.

Finding Dad in Ciudad Panama
Leahy

I was sailing as chief pumpman on a tanker owned by Victory Carriers, the U.S. flag subsidiary of Aristotle Onassis's shipping empire. We had just left Puerto Armuelles on the Pacific coast of Panama and were bound for the Panama Canal at Ciudad Panama, a trip of some twelve hours or so.

During a fire and lifeboat drill that morning, I was burned in a fire hose accident. Second degree burns from my chest to my knees, mostly on the right side of my body, it resulted from the seawater pumped to the fire hose being accidently routed through a steam heat exchanger and being just below boiling point. As soon as our ship got close enough to the Canal, I was taken ashore to the hospital in a Canal Commission launch.

For two weeks, I remained in the Clinica de San Fernando in Ciudad Panama, and endured a daily ritual of submersion in a stainless-steel whirlpool bath followed by having dead skin removed with a large tweezers by a lovely young nurse until the point when I passed out from pain.

96

The rest of the day was spent in bed watching the U.S. Army Southern Command's television station; the high points being old reruns of soap operas and adventures in bee-keeping. When the pain medication began to wear off, I simply walked down the hall to the nurses' station and repeated an Espanol phrase useful to know in this kind of situation: "Yo tengo dolor." They promptly gave me more pain meds and I was good for a few more hours.

Tanker ballasted to required canal draft, approaching Panama Canal, which means it is in the Caribbean, passing Cristobal to enter the first set of locks. Photo courtesy of Leahy.

The Clinica de San Fernando was an excellent hospital and I was treated very well. Indeed, the long-term effect of the treatment I received resulted in no typical burn scarring at all but something called "trauma of the pigmentation cells", which is to say the skin, especially in the worst area around my hip, grew back a light brown color.

The steamship agents in Panama have always been known for excellent representation, and Victor, the agent assigned to me, knew me from frequent visits to Panama at that time. He came every day to check on me, bring me cigarettes and assure me I was getting the second-best treatment in the whole country.

While I was pleasantly surprised to learn that a lowly American seaman had been placed in the second-best hospital in the whole country, I could not help but ask why I was not in the best hospital in Panama. The answer was unexpected but completely plausible.

When the Iranian revolution drove the Shah of Iran out of his palace in the dead of night, he was whisked off to a famous hospital in the U.S. for treatment of the cancer that would soon achieve what the revolutionaries had failed to do. That is to say: kill him.

But in short order it became politically untenable to continue to harbor our old puppet in the United States after our embassy in Tehran was overrun and hostages taken, so he was shipped off to our "semi-colony" of Panama. The Shah of Iran was therefore occupying the best hospital in Panama and, in the valid interests of his continued security, the entire hospital had been turned over to their one celebrated cancer patient.

All in all, I had no complaint. The Clinica de San Fernando was an excellent facility and I had no desire to be in the same place as the Shah of Iran at that stage of world affairs.

After two weeks of treatments the doctors decided that I could leave the hospital and just return for daily outpatient treatments. The agent set me up in the Hotel Internacional and had my gear, which had been taken off the ship as she transited the Canal, delivered there. I decided, however, that a stop at the Ancon Inn was called for first and directed the driver there with half my body bandaged under a loose fitting guayabera shirt and jeans.

Entering the Ancon during the day is an initially blinding experience for all involved as the bright tropical sun blasts through the door and into the very dark room where it is reflected off the mirror-covered walls. When my pupils had adjusted to the again dark light I saw at the bar, surrounded by the customary attractive young Columbian girls, the chief engineer from the *SS Star Trader*. He was also my father. I'd had no idea where he and his ship were at until this moment. Seeing the bulge of the bandages under my shirt, Dad moved in for a handshake and back pat instead of a full hug.

"Are you all right?" he asked.

"Most of the pain has eased off and I am taking pain meds, thanks. What are you doing in the Ancon Inn at eleven in the morning"?

"We docked over at Rodman (the U.S. Navy Base on the other side of the Canal) this morning and Victor came aboard and told me what had happened to you. I asked him to drive me to the hospital but he said you were being released this morning and he had a driver to take you to the Internacional. I figured after two weeks in the hospital it was more likely you would come here first."

My father knew what I would do because it is exactly what he would have done himself. I had to give up a laugh to that. I told him they were trying to repatriate me as soon as the doctor would release me but I had a good relationship with both the doctor and my agent and intended to stay in Panama as long as possible, preferably until I was fit for duty. Then I'd catch a ship coming through the Canal short-handed.

"Well you should go to our house and spend some of the recovery time with your mother. You know she won't believe you are not at death's door until she sees you herself."

Chief Engineer Mike Leahy Sr. at main engine throttles of 20,000 shaft horsepower tanker. (Author's father.) Photo courtesy Leahy.

Easy for him to say. Turns out his ship had just taken over the Navy charter that we called the romance run. This meant taking a half load of cargo and one night ashore in Curacao, transit to Aruba for the balance of the cargo and another night ashore on that island, then transit to the Canal at Colón and anchor for the next morning's convoy (with another night ashore in Colón) and then transit the Canal and stay five days (and nights!) discharging at Rodman Navy Base in Ciudad Panama. Then repeat the whole voyage again and again for a year.

"All right," I agreed. "If they make me leave the country, I will do that. Meanwhile, let's go get some lunch. They make a really good ensalada langosta at the restaurant on the roof of the Internacional and I can check in the hotel before the driver that Victor sent to nursemaid me tells him I've given him the slip."

Evita Again
Sallee

Captured by the view of the sparkling Caribbean Sea from the ship's deck nine stories up, I paused between bites of my smorgasbord lunch. Where do we stop tomorrow? This begins the "an island a day" phase of the cruise. Personally, I appreciate a day between islands so I can reflect, make a few notes and figure out what to do on the next island.

The next port is a bit of a challenge. I know it well, even have friends there. But I did not have a way to let them know I was returning. Much had occurred over the past two years. Of course, a hurricane—Category 5—political unrest sparked by a world power leader, and thousands of people fleeing.

And yes, Puerto Rico is part of the United States of America. Well, sort of, they get taxed without representation and less help than a state.

I always felt very at home here. They speak my second language—and fortunately, my first language. I am leaning toward the chance that I can go by my friends' places of work and maybe I will be lucky or providence will smile upon me.

But first, it is our friends' (Kelly and Peggy), turn to choose the tour this stop. To my disappointment, not to the city, but off to the jungle we go.

After several stops we headed back down through Rio Grande Town with billboards welcoming LGBTQ visitors, not something you often see in the rest of the good old USA. As we cruised along the coast heading to Viejo (old) San Juan, I began to plan how I could at least see Evita. I probably was not going to be able to get to Ranger Silva's station up at the Castillo San Cristobal, even if I took a cab. From the street, the entrance is still a long walk. Might be pushing it.

As we climbed down the steps of the bus, I realized we were in Columbus Square. Unbelievable. Hunger triggered by the aroma of grilled fish and vegetables made me realize it was time for lunch. Yet, at the same time I wanted to see if Evita was working at the Haitian Art Gallery, just across the plaza.

Conveniently, the Restaurante Boriken was next door. Dropping my three companions at an outdoor table, I headed for the Gallery. A glance down the bright blue ballast street stone-paved lane revealed green, yellow and azul buildings trimmed in white. Arched rough wooden doorways might lead to mystery courtyards? This was old San Juan.

Taking the two steps up through the corner entrance in one stride, I stopped to let my eyes adjust to soothing dimness. I had prepared a short statement in Spanish asking about Evita. I began reciting it before I realized it was her leaning on the counter. Her luxurious silver hair cropped back in a wave contrasting with her penetrating dark eyes above her wide smile greeted me as a long-lost brother with a tight hug. "Evita, es que tu?!"

Through her thick Bronx Spanish accent, she said "Yes, I am Eva."

"We met a few years ago and I've been wanting to meet you again. I wrote a column about you in the newspaper and now it is in my book, *Galveston Wharf Stories*," I said.

"Yes, I remember you. You asked about the people of Martinique," she said.

We spoke a while catching up when a Puerto Rican gentleman came out from the back room. Eva said, "Let me introduce you to my boss." And to him, "This is Alvin. He wrote about the Gallery in his book."

His eyebrows rose and his smile deepened. "Wonderful. If there is anything we can do, please just ask."

"May Eva come outside for a minute to see Kathy again and my friends?"

Her boss nodded, "But of course, and thank you for visiting us again."

"You have a beautiful shop and it rightfully gets very great reviews," I said.

We went outside, hugs all around. I went into the restaurant to give them my order. Eva stayed while we inhaled our delicious lunch.

And she worked only on Tuesdays—Eva with author Alvin,
another wonderful chance meeting with a friend.

I walked her back into the Gallery and bought a few small items for our granddaughters.

"I'm sorry," I said to Eva. "I thought your name was Evita."

She laughed. "It happens often; don't worry."

"If I can get your address I will mail you a copy of the book. Are you still living with your mother?"

"Yes."

"And how is she?"

"She is 95 years old and still as bright as ever. It looks like I will be staying here longer."

"How did you do with the hurricane?"

"We lost a few tiles but our house is not far from here and has survived many hurricanes."

"And how is business?"

"It is picking up a little bit. It's good because the cruise ships are returning. I am only working one day a week, Tuesdays, now."

At least I can write her that we are coming next time. And hopefully, we can outlast Covid. What were the chances that the ship I was on would come the one day of the week "Evita" worked and that she wasn't busy with another customer?

Luck or providence?

Meeting Columbus, Over & Over
Sallee

Who was Columbus?

On a bicycle tour of Freeport on Grand Bahama, led by Leroy, a proud young Black man, the descendant of slaves, we stop under an umbrella tree. Thank goodness as this 29-year-old pushed the pace. Stepping close to each of us, Leroy asked, "Who was Columbus?"

The answer: "He was the man who rediscovered the Bahamas and brought death by sword and disease. October 12th on our Island is National Heroes Day, *not* Columbus Day," Leroy stated, as he closed into our personal space looking up from his 5'6" wiry frame, black eyes fixed on ours, earnestly sharing his story, the history of the new world.

"Not really something we should celebrate," he added quietly.

Columbus's Cruises

Christopher Columbus sailed the ocean blue in 1492. Actually, he sailed on four trips, a determined man if ever there was one. His first voyage was with three ships.

In 2012, I walked aboard his ships, *La Pinta* (the painted one) and *La Nina* (the girl), in Freeport, Texas. No, not the real ones—the topical water worms got them—but hand-built replicas of the caravels, which had been used for coastal navigation in the late 1400s, not built for trans-Atlantic travel.

First impression? They were small, very small. And when you realize they had animals on board, the crew slept head to foot on the deck, and bathing was frowned upon ... even with a sea breeze, yuck.

Pinta, at 56 feet long with a beam of 17.6 feet, was the largest of the two. *Santa Maria*, the flagship, was only six feet longer.

Walking around the *Pinta*, I couldn't imagine months at sea cramped on this deck, sailing to the edge of the Earth. Back then only the educated bought Aristotle's theory that the Earth was round.

Crisscrossing the Caribbean on 1,000-foot-long cruise ships, I am amazed that someone in a small sailboat had the courage to venture forth from the sight of shore without any reference point. No doubt it took guts.

Over his four voyages, Columbus's navigational skills and equipment evolved from dead-reckoning to an early sextant, used to "shoot the stars and sun". But still, with no charts and the current and wind ... guts.

Seems that in every port you visit in the Caribbean, you meet Columbus again. The Bahamas, Cuba, Haiti and Puerto Rico, on the first voyage. Second trip, the next year, as a very religious person, Columbus named Montserrat, Antigua, Redonda, Nevis, Saint Kitts, Saint Eustatius, Saba, Saint Martin and Saint Croix, and the Virgin Islands, including Virgin Gorda—the fat virgin. Tortola and Peter Island also made the itinerary.

Third time is a charm cruise brought Columbus to Trinidad and South American. Heading back north he found Margarita, Tobago and Grenada, one of my favorites.

On his fourth and worst trip, dodging hurricanes, he landed on Martinique and Jamaica. Heading south, he tried to find China in Honduras, Nicaragua, Costa Rica and Panama, where he came within 50 miles of the Pacific Ocean, very near where the canal now exits at Colón, named for him.

Sailing back, he saw the Cayman Islands. His ships sank on the north shore of Jamaica, where he waited a year for rescue. He returned to Spain as a paying customer on a ship the next year. So, I guess that puts him in the same boat as me as a paying customer on a cruise ship.

Running to Remember

The experience with my bicycle tour-guide, Leroy, reminded me of a long run I did in 1992, 500 years after Columbus "discovered" indigenous civilizations here. A group of folks running from Alaska and another group from the tip of South America were meeting in Mexico City to remind us of the impact.

They carried medicine staffs, four-foot-long decorated walking sticks. As a marathon runner at the time, I was asked if I would go 26 miles north of Las Cruces, New Mexico, to meet them and run the staff back to town.

I was met by a white van, seats removed, quilts thrown on the metal floor. Four of us took turns running a mile, then getting in the van until our next mile. After a few miles, I said I would just keep running, giving the others a break as they had been at this for over 1,000 miles. Their tired bodies smiled.

The next day, my daughter Joan (who happens to be of Native descent) and I were invited to smoke the peace pipe in Tortugas, a small reservation nearby. We joined the circle.

The following day I was drafted to head out for El Paso, 42 miles south. I ran the whole way, often next to Tarahumara native ultra-distance (100-mile) runners from Copper Canyon, Mexico, made famous years later in the book *Born to Run.*

As we ran, they were trance-like, breathing smoothly, backs straight, eyes focused in the distance. Miles glided by as I entered an Anglo version of the trance.

Three years later, I again ran with white-robed Tarahumara men in the Shiprock Marathon. The night before they had gone to the Farmington dump where they cut running sandals from used car tires.

I even beat two of them, sort of. After all, the 26 miles we ran were just a warm up for them. I was toast.

Back to 1992. The last few miles were a sprint through downtown El Paso, cheering crowds of well-wishers shouting support as local high school cross-country teams joined in with us pushing the pace into the five-minute-a-mile range. We burst into Chamizal Park on the border of Mexico into the arms of friends and family.

A different Columbus Day celebration for sure. Still here, still proud native peoples.

End note: Please do not go see the Tarahumara folks; they need to be left alone. This was written on October 12, Columbus Day. Or as I call it: National Heroes Day, 2020—a year we celebrated our true heroes.

Singapore Surprise
Leahy

I got a call from the union dispatcher that the SS *Monroe* was on dry dock in Singapore and they needed a first engineer. The ship was due to remain in the shipyard through Christmas and New Year's, then resume her long-term charter to the Navy. She carried every sort of supplies, including munitions, between the US Navy bases at Guam, Subic Bay in the P.I. (Philippines), and Diego Garcia out in the middle of the Indian Ocean.

When I arrived at Keppel's Shipyard in Singapore I found the captain to be Carlo, an old acquaintance from Galveston. An exceptional individual, he had graduated from the Texas Maritime Academy with a 3rd mate's license, gone to sea, and raised his license to Captain. Then he returned to the Academy, taking the engineering courses and again graduated with a 3rd engineer's license before proceeding to go to sea again, raising his engineering license to chief engineer.

There are very few mariners to be found who hold both unlimited master and unlimited chief engineer licenses. Carlo had been on this ship for several years and the ship had been on this Navy charter on the same run for a number of years, as well. He sailed for four-month tours of duty, which was typical for all of us at that time, and his relief was another captain who was from Texas and a Texas Maritime Academy graduate. Carlo was scheduled to be relieved and to go home to Galveston on vacation when the shipyard repairs were over. The ship would then resume her normal voyage route with a new captain.

Eventually, we were finally able to coax this old ship into something resembling seaworthiness and demonstrate that to the attending USCG marine inspectors based in the Singapore inspection office. The American Bureau surveyor was also satisfied to re-issue the ship's various class certificates, as well.

Author Leahy's last ship, breakbulk freighter SS Cleveland drops anchor in Singapore. Photo courtesy of Leahy.

After the briefest of sea trials, cut short due to the pressing need for the ship to get to Guam and an approaching tropical storm, the returning captain relieved Carlo. We headed right into the teeth of a typhoon and pounded our way to the passage through the Philippine Islands and onward to Guam. It was over a week before any of the engineers got more than a couple of hours sleep or even left the engine room.

There have been pirates operating in the Straits of Malacca since time immemorial. This ship had been boarded and the captain's safe robbed twice in past years while transiting the Straits, so we now took a series of ship-hardening precautions.

Down below, I raised the boilers up to maximum steam generation and increased the ship's speed accordingly. One off-watch officer and crew member were positioned on the fantail with shotguns and .45 caliber handguns to repel boarders from following speed boats (the usual approach). A similar team was set up on the flying bridge to defend the wheelhouse. Steel frames were lowered at each outside deck ladderway to prevent anyone who did get aboard from coming up from the main deck to the bridge, and all exterior openings to the inside of the ship were locked or secured with steel bars. The pirates made no further successful attacks after these measures were taken.

We arrived back at Singapore about a month later. After I had been relieved, I took a shower, donned some light clothing considering the serious heat and humidity in Singapore and headed to the Terror Club for a cold beer. (The humidity in Singapore is such that the wet hair I had after showering was still wet when I returned to the ship hours later. The sensation made me feel like I could push the water in the air out of the way when walking forward.)

As I passed by the big swimming pool, with various people doing laps in the water, I heard my name called out. Not that unusual until I saw who was hailing me from a lounge chair. It always takes me a minute to adjust when I see a face I know well but in a completely unexpected context. This was Carlo, the captain who had headed home to Galveston weeks ago for four months of vacation.

"Captain! Good to see you my friend, but what are you doing here? I thought you went back Stateside a month ago."

"Well, after y'all sailed, I decided to go visit the P.I. for a while instead of going home, and then I decided to come back here and hang out in Singapore for a while, as well. Not sure when I'll get around to going home. Maybe I'll just stay out here until it's time to go back to work."

Thinking I may have inadvertently wandered into personal matters, I decided to quit asking questions. When asking about our lifestyle of world travel and extended time away from home, friends ashore on occasion have told me that they assumed that seamen tend to not be married.

That is not the case. In fact, nearly all seamen I have known have been married but, for most of us, we have been married more than once. It is a difficult lifestyle for wives and not everyone is adaptable to it.

"Well anyway, it's good to see you," I said. Come on up to the terrace and have a Tiger beer."

Get Off My Island
Sallee

That morning, I had not taken two steps on Martinique before a heated argument ensued with a descendent of slaves, now forced to cater to tourists. He began a loud argument over the exchange rate and concluded by ordering me off "his island". It appeared as if he needed to exercise power over someone, even a bewildered tourist.

I walked around a few blocks before heading back to the ship. No money spent. I wondered why those folks were so bitter and unhappy, or was it me?

I began to interview returning fellow passengers about their experiences ashore. All except one said they wouldn't come back. The local people had been awful to them. The sea brings us together for better or worse.

The one passenger who enjoyed the visit, a large, redheaded 20-something guy, had hired a cab to take him to every bar on Front Street. Unsteady on his feet, slurring his speech he declared, "Martinique was the best stop."

On our next island, Puerto Rico, I found people enjoying life. I had asked a middle-aged saleswoman, Evita, why people in Martinique were so unfriendly. She replied that they had a miserable history and seemed to be permanently sad.

When confronted by unhappy folks I challenge myself to get them to smile. Basically, I believe people are good even though they don't always act that way. Make that "we" don't always ...

Now two years later, I was about to return to Martinique, and given my first experience and Evita's assessment, I decided to study their history. It wasn't difficult to see why they would be angry. Their ancestors were kidnapped from Africa, enslaved, sold and families broken up. By the time they were freed, the sugar cane economy had collapsed, leaving only poverty.

From the upper deck, I paused as we docked, watching the small ripple pattern on the surface of the deep blue sea blown by a gentle wind toward the violent Mt. Pele, wrapped in shades of grey clouds. Waters which hosted the Battle of the Straits, a 1779 clash of massive wooden sailing ships blasted by 32-pound cannonballs, splitting and shooting wood daggers through sailors, decapitating others. Blood soaked the sand and spread on the decks. The British prevailed over the French. Later the British traded the island back to the French as part of the treaty ending a war far away in Europe.

The Revolutionary French freed 100,000 slaves on the island only to have Napoléon enslave them again 20 years later. His beautiful dark-skinned Martinique-born wife, Josephine, stood next to him. Revolts ensued and finally the slaves were freed in 1848, years before Lincoln did in the U.S.A.

By 1902, the city of Saint-Pierre, the major city on the Island, was known as "the Paris of the Caribbean". Then in a split second, 30,000 of Martinique's citizens were killed in by a violent volcano blast. Saint-Pierre was no more.

Then came the World War II experience, portrayed Humphrey Borgart-style in the movie *To Have and Have Not*. Martinique citizens continued living as second-rate citizens of France, a million miles away.

The next invasion was by American tourists—some of them Ugly Americans. When these tourists come to Galveston, I sometimes get mad too.

In 1991, in the Fort-d-France town square park, someone chopped off the statue of Josephine's head. One could guess that the Martinique citizens were about to revolt again. If white

Americans had been treated like this, believe me, the French would have been overthrown long ago. Or Texas-fashion, Martinique would secede.

I quietly walked off the gangway down through the streets to a park on the tourist route. I sat on a bench and observed the Martinique folks go about their daily life, setting up tents, as tourists streamed into their community. Clearly a descendent of African slaves, a gentleman approached me, his head topped with a colorful Rasta hat.

As if a circus performer, he had beaded necklaces everywhere. He asked me if I was interested in buying some for my lady friend. As I was alone, I assume this was a standard question when engaging a potential male customer.

I showed an interest, and then began asking him open-ended questions about his life on Martinique. He maintained a large, white-toothed smile as I examined the bracelets and he told his story, a story I could not even begin to imagine.

His life goals were universal. Maslow's Needs Hierarchy, basic needs for his family including security, happiness and love for his children and hope that they have a better life.

I bought two sets of bracelets and necklaces for my granddaughters. (I knew they would probably disappear soon after they looked at them, and I was correct.) But it was worth the few dollars for a valuable lesson from Martinique's "Fred".

Stars and Stripes in St. Maarten
Sallee

"Do you want to do another 15-day cruise?" she asked.

"Where does it go?" I inquired.

"Eastern Caribbean."

"Does it go to St. Maarten?"

"Why do you want to go there again?"

"Because Tom and Ian aren't in Cozumel anymore since hurricane Irma destroyed the boats in St. Maarten. So, the owner moved the Cozumel America's Cup Regatta there."

"Ah … yes, we do stop there. Why didn't you go sailing last time we were in St. Maarten?"

"Because I went to Moho beach with Steve. Boy, was that stupid, standing 20 feet from the end of the runway in the sand while huge 747 jet wheels passed three feet over our heads."

"This trip I want the speed of a fast 12-metre boat. Tom and Ian should be there. We raced a half dozen times in Cozumel and I beat Tom last time."

Before I knew it, a few months later, the cruise ship eased up to St. Maarten wharf. A dash across the gangway through the always-there chain-store tourist traps to where I could finally embrace the real smells and sights of the Island.

I walked down Juancho Yrausquin Boulevard into Phillipsburg. Not a "boulevard" like Broadway in Galveston, it's named for a politician who called the Dutch islands together to demand independence. Well, he got them to where they are now, sort of a commonwealth.

History lesson aside, I sensed another fine morning to sail. Approaching was an attractive, middle-aged woman dressed in a form-fitting seersucker suit, at least two-inch heels, all topped by a Hepburn-style hat over her elegant hairdo. She smiled at me as she swayed pass. The tune *The Girl from Ipanema* flowed through me. Maybe from the other side? Was I staring? Probably.

By the "other side" one means the other side of the island, St. Martin, which is everything French. Straight from Paris—food, language, shops—mixed with colonial past. Old history still at peace after all these years.

More recent history is found down the street at the small shop with a model of the *Stars & Stripes* hull out front. This is the place.

With a group of about 16 tourists, we were efficiently processed, divided into teams and trained during our barge trip out to the sailboats. Asked if we wanted to be observers, active or very active, the division of labor is set for crew members. Usually, I said active, but today I said very active as I was going to be racing with one of the brothers.

Slowing, we arrived at the sailboats. I noticed no Tom or Ian. As I stepped aboard *Stars & Stripes* a good-sized white 30-

something gentleman boomed, "Welcome aboard, I'm Captain Morgan."

Really? Oh well, this is a tourist gig. Sure his name is Morgan.

"So, do you want to be our midship grinder?" he asked.

Now trapped, I answer, "Yes, that's okay."

We cast off our mooring and began to practice—a young focused crew, including two big, motivated guys on the main grinder which requires two such people for success.

Knowing we were on a fast clock for the start, I didn't ask about the missing brothers.

I took up my position, grabbed the handles and began to practice turning them in one direction and then back in the other at the command of the captain. This was a step up in required strength from my usual aft grinder position. No sitting down on this job.

Captain Morgan maneuvered us out in the bay toward the imaginary start line. He muttered a running commentary, like a stage whisper, and it built suspense. A false start almost certainly will lose the race. A bit of quick wiggling of the helm saved us from crossing the line too early, but it also slowed us down. We had a slight lead as the Canadian boat jerked towards the line just missing us.

We had the wind in our sails, which blocked theirs, and we shot forward. The bow quartered through clear three-foot waves like a knife through a ripe watermelon as a bit of spray misted over us.

Intensively focused on my job, I translated the captain's shouted commands into lay person terms, then thought through each arm motion while trying not to fall out of the boat. No muscle memory. In a flash, the 45-minute race, was over and the captain shouted congrats to all of us on a job well done.

I looked around for the Canadian boat. It was far aft. Largest victory ever for me.

"So how are Tom and Ian doing?" I asked. "And is their sister still a captain of that large sailboat in the Mediterranean? And Dad still racing around Grenada?"

Captain Morgan sat back and looked at me with his head cocked to one side. He paused, and then asked, "How do you know this family so well?"

"Well I've raced with them about eight or nine times in Cozumel. And I put them in a book I wrote about wharf stories. They are an amazing family and the fact that each of the kids was born on a different continent tells you they really did grow up touring the whole world on a sailboat."

Then he said, "Let me ring them up." He did this on a satellite phone, and I enjoyed visiting with Tom and Ian for a few minutes—they had indeed moved to St. Maarten but were visiting their dad in Grenada.

Capt. Morgan talked a minute and hung up. I wondered what the call had cost.

"Would you like to take the helm?" he asked. The brothers know the real reason I sail, to feel the thrill of guiding this massive boat through the water. They had suggested to Capt. Morgan to let me drive a while.

"Yes!" I answer, not ashamed at my kid-like eagerness. "What course would you like?" I asked.

"Oh, just head towards the blue hotel on the beach, that's good."

About 15 minutes later while still way offshore I asked, "Where now?"

"You can sail over by the cruise ships then out to the start line then back toward the hotel."

The start line? The one I didn't see because I was focused on the handles? Maybe, out by the rocky point.

I steered that direction, passing the two huge cruise ships. Passengers at the rails waved. For a second, I am Dennis Connor bringing home the Cup.

Now toward the point. No alarm sounded from the captain so far, so I guessed I was on course.

Then I heard a gentle, "Bring her down about ten points." Message: You are heading too close toward the rocks.

Guiding this sailboat is like flying a jet compared to our solid but far less swift sailboats at Sea Star Base Galveston. While I didn't get to see Tom and Ian in person, I am sure Captain Morgan filled them in on what I am up to.

I like this way of communicating—from the deck of *Stars & Stripes*.

Oh, and his name really is Morgan.

Author Sallee at the helm of the America's Cup winner, Stars & Stripes. Note the competing boat behind, over his right shoulder.

Unexpected meeting in Hong Kong
Leahy

In the mid 1980s, I was on vacation from my permanent 2nd engineer's position on a tanker when I got a call to do a short-term consulting job. I joined the ship in San Pedro intending to try to complete the survey before her final Far East port call. I'd then get off and join the sister ship in Hong Kong or Japan and do the survey on her during her return voyage to the US. I ended up getting off the first ship in Hong Kong with several days to kill before learning from the local agent when and where I could join the second ship.

I found my way to a couple of bars I knew in Kowloon: Ned Kelly's, where any Australians in town tended to congregate, and the Bottoms Up Club, frequented by expat Americans and Europeans.

The Bottoms Up Club's big claim to fame was that it was featured in a scene in a James Bond film. I forget which one, might have been the *Man with the Golden Gun*. An interesting place downstairs from street level, it consists of a series of individual rooms hung with tapestries, heavy on velvet material, with a circular bar in each room.

Inside the circle of each bar sits an attractive young lady on a riser, serving as bartender. These girls are topless. The clientele tends to be either foreigners or local gentlemen conducting business negotiations with the foreigners.

With the lease turnover of Hong Kong from the British to the People's Republic of China just a few years away, many American businessmen were in evidence, no doubt trying to get an early foothold in place with mainland Chinese representatives. The place was abuzz with capitalist deal making.

With some effort, I managed to convince one of the lovely bartenders that she should serve as my guide and temporary girlfriend during my time in Hong Kong.

Accordingly, the following afternoon she and I were sitting at a table in the lobby bar of the Sheraton enjoying a bottle of San Miguel, an exceptionally good beer made in the Philippines. While I was telling her some no doubt enhanced version of my life story, I heard someone close by say my name.

"Mike, is that you, Mike?"

I looked up at a tall young man standing over us and while his face was remarkably familiar, I could not for the life of me connect where I knew him from in the context of our present location. Fortunately, my confusion did not last so long as to be embarrassing. It was my own cousin, who the last I knew was still living in the New York metropolitan area from whence the American-born members of our family, including myself, originate.

He was not a seaman and I could not think of any logical reason for him to be standing there now. We had not seen each other in several years.

"Dean, it's great to see you, but what in world are you doing in Hong Kong?"

"I'm here with the IMF. We're on a trade mission in the Far East. We go from here to Singapore in a few days and then, believe it or not, we move on to Vietnam."

"IMF as in the International Monetary Fund? Like, David Rockefeller and such?"

Dean was an aviation engineer specializing in helicopters, but he worked also with fixed-wing aircraft. The last I knew he had been working for Petroleum Helicopter Inc. doing maintenance on their choppers on the Gulf Coast. I'd heard he was back in the New York area, I just didn't know who he was working for.

"Yeah, I got a job running all the maintenance and repair work for the IMF's fleet of aircraft last year and well, here I am. I am traveling with Mr. Rockefeller and his staff as part of the flight crew to maintain the plane during the trip."

"Well I'll be damned. It is truly a small world— there could not possibly be a more random meeting than this."

I'd already had my evening planned out for me by my Chinese girlfriend. I was scheduled to take her, along with her elderly mother and whichever other family members chose to tag along, to dinner at what I was sure would be an expensive restaurant, even by Hong Kong price standards. I invited Dean to join us, which he did, and big night on the town in Hong Kong was had by all.

A high point for me during dinner came after the waiters had placed a platter with a huge, whole, fish in the center of the large round table. It was supposed to be sea bass. To my understanding, sea bass was simply a more attractive name given by marketers for Patagonian toothfish, but since we were a hell of a long way from Chile, I presume it was indeed a sea bass.

The girl's mother, of an indeterminable age somewhere between 80 and 150 years young, reached across to the center of the table and carefully plucked the eyeball from the fish and popped it in her mouth, aiming a guilty smile in my direction. And while I had certainly seen fish eyeball eaten before and knew it to be considered a delicacy, I had never seen the act performed with such grace and speed as the old lady displayed.

Author Leahy had chance meetings around the world. This is Shipbreaker's Yard outside Karachi, Pakistan. Photo courtesy of Leahy.

A Pirate in St. Croix
Sallee

"Pepsi or Coke?"

Our cruise line had just switched to Pepsi—yuck and politically incorrect in our family. Mother had a Coke every afternoon at 4 o'clock for all of her 94 years. Father-in-law ran the St. Louis Coke plant and distant relatives owned Coca-Cola. In fact, my wife and I got a large silver tray as a wedding present from them on which during graduate school we ate our peanut butter sandwiches.

As we disembarked at St. Croix in the U.S. Virgin Islands, we had two missions. First, get to the other end of the Island to

Christiansted to see the sights. Second, was to find and purchase all of the Diet Coke we could carry.

As with many places I have imagined throughout the years, the real experience can range from a slap in the face, to punch to the stomach. Hollywood and Vine, Times Square, the Alamo ... you get the idea.

Now I can add St. Croix to the list. Expecting what I later learned was St. Lucia with lush green mountains raising from the turquoise sea while hoisting bright white sails, St. Croix was not. Reality was being jammed into a van after being herded through a narrow street. We drove down Centerline Road across the 22-mile-long island arriving in a congested area. Like being spun around on a bat, we were disoriented and unloaded in "downtown" Christiansted.

Interaction with not too friendly or helpful folks finally got me in the general area of the Old Scale House on Hospital street. Clearly, the local folks tried to put together displays but the amateur efforts had me back to the van pick up point early.

Besides wanting to be back in Fredrikstad, we needed to find those Diet Cokes. Being sure to wedge myself in the van so I could view the other side of the island, I soon wondered if I'd gotten mixed up. The same, almost lunarscape stared back at me all the way across the Island.

Back in Market Square, a rectangle the size of a tennis court, by the way, I tried to stretch and straighten my legs so I could walk again. Funneled through the historic path towards the pier we came to Front Street, the last one before the water. With St. Patrick Church to the right, the only option for a store was to turn left into a small mob of returning tourists from excursions.

The front bumper of a very old beat-up pickup truck had crept up to my butt. So, I stepped up on a very high curb, a Galveston Strand-style high curb. I looked down and saw diving tanks and fins in a barrel in the back of the pickup. Made sense, the overhead sign just ahead read *Adventures in Diving*.

Below me, still on street level, was a short guy with the large brim all-around sailing cap. Talking through his hat's brim a question emerged.

"Are you a passenger on that cruise ship?"

"Yes," came my reply.

"Where is it out of?"

"Galveston, believe it or not," I stated.

"Wow, I'm from Houston," said the brim.

"Come on, no one is just from Houston. Where?"

He chuckled. "Okay, Kemah."

From the voice, I gathered there was some age on this guy. "Are you retired?"

"Sort of. I run sunset sailboat trips."

I exclaimed, "Capt. Joe (Stumpf), is that you?"

Looking up for the first time to where I could see his face, he said, "Hey, you're that reporter."

He turned to his friend. "This guy did a good story on Capt. Kidd a few years ago." (Capt. Kidd is a custom built "pirate" boat—skull and bones flag and arrggh!!—as it says in the taped safety briefing.) "We sailed down here last week," he continued. "We just came over here to Fredrikstad today to see which cruise ship was coming in."

I laughed. "That's funny. We went to the other end of the Island to see the sights."

Then it struck me, was this island so boring to this bigger than life guy, that he had to come look at our standard run of the mill cruise ship for something to do? After all, Capt. Joe had sailed in small boats around the Caribbean and across the Gulf of Mexico like most of us walk to the park.

"How is Nadine doing?" I inquired.

"Oh, she's fine; she is a great asset. I imagine she'll be a lifelong sailor. She's on the *Elissa* crew now too and takes the Tall Ship of Texas out when they sail."

"Tell her hello for me," I asked him, remembering her having gone from a musician passenger to first mate.

"Sure, she'll remember you from being in the newspaper."

"And the first woman J/Boat coach on the Chesapeake Bay?" I asked.

"Oh, you mean Koralina—we call her Koral. Still there, but she realized she was strictly in a man's world up there and any further advancement as a coach would not be possible. In fact, they even told her that. Anyway, after that she made an Atlantic crossing and then sailed to Hawaii. She married a few years back, turned her career to teaching and owns her own boat.

"By the way," he continued, "We moved *Capt. Kidd* over the bridge to Seabrook—better spot."

The Capt. Kidd relaxes dockside after another wonderful music-filled sunset cruise. Ahh ...

We agreed this was really something, seeing each other by chance so far from home. We caught up on each other's lives and he told me where to find Diet Cokes. As we parted, we promised to go sailing whenever Capt. Joe got back to Seabrook.

Then COVID hit. Still waiting till I can get back to Seabrook, after all, the *Kidd* has begun sailing again.

P.S. We did find the Diet Cokes. They were selling so fast at the small market, you paid inside and went out to the truck and told the guy how many cases you paid for and he gave them to you.
Trusting, nice folks, after all. Pirates really do know their way around the Caribbean.

Unrelated Uncles and USS Boxer
Sallee

The USS *Boxer* (CV-21) left San Francisco in July, 1950, heading to Japan and on to the Korea theater. *Boxer*, an Essex-class aircraft carrier, was loaded to the gills with P-51 fighter aircraft parked everywhere, even on the elevators. The planes were desperately needed for the new conflict. *Boxer* set a record for the shortest crossing of the Pacific, on the Great Circle route, eight days, seven hours. Come to find out, my Uncle Wally wasn't the only uncle on that trip.

In 2021, my wife Kathy's Aunt Emma Lea read the story about Uncle Wally and *Boxer* in my book, *Galveston Wharf Stories,* and immediately called.

Aunt Emma Lea's uncle, Elmer A. Rice, was a naval aviator and on the *Boxer* that same trip. He would fly P-51s in Korea. Both men were Navy lieutenants aboard the ship with a crew of 3,440 and over 1,000 "passengers."

So, did the uncles meet? Aviators were part of the crew, the elite of the elite, riding escalators up to lounge chairs in an air-conditioned ready room. Uncle Wally was a "passenger." My guess is they probably didn't, but who knows? Uncle Wally was an engaging guy.

Uncle Wally got off *Boxer* in Japan where he was rushed aboard USS *Remora* (SS-487), a World War II-style submarine. *Remora* immediately sailed to protect *Boxer* and other surface ships from possible attacks from Chinese ships off the Korean coast.

When *Boxer* arrived, Uncle Elmer's assignment was to fly defensive patterns to protect U.S. ships from enemy jets. He flew the best World War II propeller plane against the enemy's new Russian jets. After gaining the sky from the enemy, his squadron flew low-level, close-support missions for U.S. troops as they went ashore at Inchon and then drove inland to recapture Seoul, Korea's capital city.

In November, while Uncle Elmer was flying a mission, *Boxer* slowed to 26 knots due to an engine problem. A key reduction gear failed, largely because *Boxer* had skipped its regular maintenance in the haste to get the P-51s to Korea. *Boxer* received orders to return to San Diego to make repairs, returning to the battle five months later.

On one of his 80 missions, over a two-year span, Uncle Elmer's plane was hit by Chinese flak outside a large seaport. The plane's engine stopped during the second bombing run, shooting flames back into the cockpit, searing his face and lower arms. He bailed out of his spinning plane over the beach, and while wounded, he dragged his small rubber raft out through the surf into the sea. Later he was pulled up into a Navy helicopter.

Surviving his time in the Korean conflict, even after being shot down with injuries, Uncle Elmer remained in the Navy, finishing his degree at the University of Kansas. After service on subs in Korea, Uncle Wally stayed in the Navy too.

In 1956, as a Navy pilot out of San Diego, Uncle Elmer was testing a new weapon, an air-to-air, heat-seeking missile. Exactly what happened is not easily found. But with family lore and some data, it appears after firing the missile from his *Panther* jet, the missile reversed course and fixed on Uncle Elmer's plane. Trying to dodge it, Uncle Elmer twisted his jet, as did the missile, finally blowing up his plane.

This was not the only fatality due to wayward missiles in the early days. But this was the one that affected Kathy's family.

Elmer A. Rice

Uncle Wally survived 14 crossings of the Pacific as a Navy signalman aboard Merchant Marine ships, second only to the Marines as the most dangerous, deadliest service during World War II.

He commanded the *Albacore*, an experimental submarine, and captained a submarine out of Key West during the Cuban Missile Crisis. After serving as a nuclear submarine squadron captain, he worked in D.C., at times briefing the White House.

Uncle Wally was happy that he was never assigned to the Pentagon. It was interesting, though, that each spring he often had Tuesday and Friday "afternoon meetings" at the Pentagon. But by then his navigational skills must have been slipping as he would get "lost" yet somehow miraculously end up at all of my cousin Kenny's baseball games.

Capt. Wallace A. Greene died at age 94 and will be interred at the Arlington National Cemetery. He will join Lt. Elmer A. Rice. Maybe they will finally meet. After all, it's a small world.

Why are you in Mombasa?
Leahy

One afternoon in the 1970s, I was walking up the hill from the wharves on Kilindini Road in Mombasa, Kenya. I had been in port there for a week or so at the time and was headed to the veranda of the Castle Hotel for sundowners. This hotel was (and probably still is) like a still frame from an old 1930's film about the British in their tropical colonies. In fact, it had only been 20 years or so since Kenya had been a British East Africa colony.

As I approached the decorative giant steel elephant tusks that form arches over both sides of Kilindini Road—a divided boulevard with grassy esplanade in the center—I caught up to a small group of Masai who were headed in the same direction as me. As is their habit, they were walking slowly in the center of the automobile lanes, haughtily ignoring the frustrated drivers trying to maneuver around them.

Wearing the traditional clothing of a bright red toga-like garment, with their hair braided with red clay, barefoot, and covered with jewelry, they were a striking sight. Especially considering the large spears they carried. This was no sort of special event, just a group of Masai walking to some destination while in town.

As I got within a block of the Castle Hotel, I could see the usual group of beggars on the sidewalk adjacent to the veranda. In general, beggars in Africa are often tragic sights of crippled people, but in Mombasa I encountered the most extreme examples. I have been told parents intentionally break the bones of some of their children when they are babies which results in terrible forms of crippling but provides the family with income.

I would really like to believe this story is false, but if you see the crippled beggars of Mombasa you will be hard-pressed to understand how else they could have come to be so damaged. Shoemakers fashion custom leather sandals to fit the parts of their bodies that are in contact with the sidewalk and ground, commonly the sides of their knees, ankles and elbows. It is a terrible sight and certainly one to raise sympathy for their plight. We always allow a few shillings to give to them.

Approaching me through the crowd on the sidewalk I spotted a familiar face, albeit not one I had any reason to expect to see that afternoon. Sal was a former shipmate and friend from Galveston. He and I had met some years earlier in Galveston's Palace Club on Postoffice Street, and the good woman who owned that den of seamen, longshoremen, professional gamblers, and off-duty peace officers served as a surrogate mother to many seafarers, included both Sal and myself.

He was an AB and had been on the same ship I was currently on but had gotten off in New Orleans before we sailed foreign. Something about needing to take care of some personal matter before leaving the country for several months. "I thought we left you behind in New Orleans man. How'd you get here?" I asked him.

"Good to see you too. I caught another ship a few days after you sailed and I guess we caught up with you at some point along the coast here. I need some help, Mike. Our bo'sn got himself arrested last night and I need to get up a tarpaulin muster to get him out of the local can. I was just over at the police station and the jail is horrible. They have little kids in there with the adult men. They have guys from different tribes together in there together too, and that seems to be a problem. The conditions are filthy beyond belief."

A "tarpaulin muster" is an old seaman's expression for getting the crew to all contribute some money for a pressing cause. Getting a shipmate out of jail was, unfortunately, a common example. It dates to a time when cargo hold hatch covers were not hydraulically operated for quick and easy opening and closing. When in port during cargo operations, the hatches were removed to elsewhere on the deck and a large tarpaulin was secured over the cargo hold when it rained or when a particular hold was not in use for a period of time. Crewmembers literally tossed what money they had onto the tarp.

"What have they arrested him for?"

"He was buying an "arm" of weed and failed to see a policeman watching the whole transaction. I asked the sergeant at the desk what I had to do to get him released and he told me it was a simple matter of giving him a thousand shillings."

An "arm" was the local package size of marijuana. Being approximately a quarter-kilo and wrapped in newspaper, it resembled a man's forearm.

"That's not too bad, less than a hundred bucks. I can throw in a hundred shillings myself. Depending on how much you have, I think we should go over to the Seaman's Club. There should be some of the crew from my ship and yours there and some others, as well. Probably be able to raise contributions there quickest."

The Seaman's Club in Mombasa was a fairly good one, a fine old building with big windows on the front wall looking out over the port. A stand-up, marble topped, bar and usually a unique assortment of local ladies wearing western-style mini-skirts and colorful wigs. Depending on how long a man had been at sea, they could seem either comical or quite attractive.

In short order, we had raised the money to get Sal's bo'sn out of jail. Not only had the American seamen in the Club pitched in but a few Brits were there and they added their contributions as well. Brotherhood of the Sea. I guess this money could be seen as either a fine or a bribe, depending on what happened to it after we handed it over to the desk sergeant, but that was not our concern.

One seldom experiences the depth of gratitude a brother seafarer can develop when you spring him out of an East African jail, but the bo'sn obviously had no money left to buy us a beer, his money having disappeared when he was arrested. Also, he needed to get back to his ship anyway and explain to the mate why he had failed to turn to that morning, so Sal and I proceeded to my original goal: sundowners at the Castle Hotel.

Sitting on that tiled and white columned veranda, with huge, slow turning ceiling fans and potted palms and ferns all around, it was relatively cool in the equatorial heat of early evening. With the waiter, barefoot and dressed in white linen tunic, loose black, shin-length trousers and a red fez with tassel bringing the cold Tusker beer from the bar, one could imagine oneself as a minor character in one of the those old "British in the Tropics" films of a few decades back.

The big show occurred each day at dusk when the colony of fruit bats that lived in the massive tree in the esplanade across from the front of the hotel emerged from the branches and headed out for their dinner. These were huge bats, perhaps 18 inches of wingspan, and it was really something to see. Mombasa was always one of my favorite ports.

CHAPTER 6
Sea War Stories

In This Chapter
Sallee

The sea has always been a main stage for war. Even the development of passenger ships, such as the *SS United States,* was influenced by the need to transport the military.

The U.S.A, as a large country with three coasts, has always turned to the deep blue waters to protect and to transit troops and supplies to far off clashes. Galveston as a critical port has witnessed many fitting outs, such as for the USS *Stewart* and actions including Torpedoes in the Gulf. All of which means there are sea stories to be told.

Here are personal accounts of the Greatest Generation, who are leaving us every day, and the experiences of the men and women who restored a World War II destroyer escort and as you will see in the next chapter, submarines. We captured as many tales of their heroic adventures as we could to include in these chapters.

Chief Rudy Biro, an original crew member on USS *Stewart*, has allowed us to publish never before seen photos of *Stewart* in combat during World War II along with his stories. And 2nd class sonarman, Neal Van Dussen, is still telling detail descriptions of WWII kamikaze attacks off Okinawa.

You are now piped aboard.

Memorial to Naval Hero
Sallee

Standing on the newly painted deck next to the capstan on the bow, thirty feet above the water while looking out at Bolivar Roads, the memory jumps to my mind.

A huge white 1963 Ford Galaxy station wagon speeds through the New Mexico desert. Two 40-ish women in front and eight kids from 14 to four years old (seven boys and one tough girl) are scattered throughout the rest of the "boat".

Voices, not exactly musical, belt out, *From the halls of Montezuma to the shores of Tripoli ...* and *Anchors aweigh my boys ...* blast from our lips. My cousins and I are singing every Armed Services hymn we can think of. At least we get the words correct.

Little did I dream that 55 years later I would be on the deck of the third ship named for the man who actually lived the origins of those two hymns, Rear Admiral Charles Stewart.

As the fleet commander in 1803, he oversaw the landing of the first U.S. Marines on the African shores of Tripoli. Barges with U.S. Naval personnel sneaked into the harbor, burning the captured frigate USS *Philadelphia*, destroying it so the enemy could not make use of it. These actions paved the way to victory in the Barbary Wars, the first U.S. war after the American Revolution.

The last of eight children, Stewart went to sea on a merchant ship as a cabin boy at age 12. Commissioned as a lieutenant at age 19, the month before the U.S. Navy was formerly founded, he was the longest serving Naval officer in history. As late as 1869, from his death bed at age 91, he advised President Lincoln on ship deployments for the blockade of the South during the Civil War, including how to keep supplies out of Galveston.

After 55 years in the Navy, he was just in mid-career, and here I am retired, recalling childhood memories, standing on the ship named for this famous captain of "Old Ironsides", the USS *Constitution.* Still on active duty in Boston, it's the only ship to outlive Stewart.

During the War of 1812, he commanded USS *Constellation*, the sister ship. A wonderful large-scale model is located in the Galveston Historical Museum. It is well worth a trip to see the decks this great officer walked while again defeating the strongest Navy in the world at the time, the British.

Back to the 75-year-old steel deck on which I stand, it was brought back to life through the hard work of volunteers and the next great generation, Texas A&M at Galveston cadets, first under the guidance of Master Chief Ross Garcia and now Retired Chief Aric Deuel.

For those in the Galveston area: If you want to walk the decks of USS Stewart and maybe scrape some rust—it never sleeps—just email the Galveston Naval Museum. They'll sign you up for Work Week and you too can sing some well-known tunes.

USS Stewart
Sallee

USS *Stewart*, a destroyer escort (DE 238), was laid down in 1942 on Greens Bayou, Houston, Texas, just 50 miles from her home today. She was the first ship built in this new shipyard on the muddy banks of the bayou. Her plates were used as templates for all other DE's produced in that yard.

She was outfitted in Galveston and commissioned May, 1943. Under command of LCDR B. C. Turner, USNR, *Stewart* began service operating out of Miami as a "school ship" training student officers.

She escorted President Roosevelt in the presidential yacht down the Potomac River to rendezvous with USS *Iowa* in Chesapeake Bay for his secret mission to Casablanca and Tehran. *(See Chief Biro's adventures on her later in this chapter.)*

In 1944, she commenced North Atlantic convoy operations, making 30 crossings with occasional enemy submarine and aircraft encounters. Heavy seas and icing conditions were frequent.

In April, 1945, *Stewart* came to the rescue of the flaming gasoline tanker, SS *Saint Mihiel*. The *Stewart* and part of the *Mihiel* crew put out the fires, saving the ship.

Stewart moved into the Pacific theater in July, 1945, where she was briefly used to conduct training exercises out of Pearl Harbor. *Stewart* was escorting a large convoy toward Japan when news came of Japan's surrender. The convoy made a perfectly curved 180-degree turn and headed back to the U.S.

She was decommissioned in January, 1947. In 1974, *Stewart* was formally donated to Seawolf Park. She is the third ship named for Rear Admiral Charles Stewart who commanded another ship in the historic naval fleet, USS *Constitution*, from 1813 to 1815.

Charles Stewart was born in Philadelphia, PA, on 28 July 1778. He went to sea in 1791 at the age of twelve as a cabin boy and rose through the ranks years to rear admiral. In the war of 1812, he also commanded *Argus*, *Hornet* and *Constellation*. He took the *Constitution* through two brilliant cruises as captain. Commodore Stewart served the Navy in some capacity for 78 years.

USS *Stewart* appears on the list of National Register of Historical Places.

*After 75 years, Chief Rudy Biro again stands at his
starboard side watch station aboard USS Stewart.*

Original Crew Member of USS Stewart
Sallee

Hanging over the front of the pulpit, I stretched far over. No, it was not Sunday, and no, I was not in church preaching. I was on USS *Stewart's* top deck, 50 feet up in a lookout platform painting the antenna platform below.

This was a special day. Chief Gunner's Mate Rudy Biro, a plank owner on the USS *Stewart*, was coming back aboard. He was traveling all the way from Maryland just as he did in 1943—this time with his family.

Soon I heard a yell, "The Chief's here!" Scrambling down, I joined Chief Biro on the second deck up where almost exactly 75 years before he manned his station as a gunnery chief. I gladly sat down on hard steel to visit. This time he was in a lawn chair—no sitting when he served.

Beginning at the beginning, he said he was born by the Naval Shipyard in D.C.

I exclaimed, "Oh, you were born in Anacostia."

He looked at me with renewed interest. "Yes, I was," he replied.

I explained, "As a baby we lived there while Dad was at sea".

Rudy Biro joined the naval reserves while in high school for the summer cruises and monthly stipend. He was called to active duty a year before Pearl Harbor was attacked.

Aboard USS *George F. Elliott*, a transport ship, Rudy had fallen three decks when a board he was standing on broke. After being in a coma with broken bones for 30 days, he joined USS *Hamul*, a destroyer escort tender. Meanwhile, USS *Elliott* was sunk by the Nazi's. He was assigned to a brand-new destroyer escort.

Arriving too early in Galveston to join the new USS *Stewart*, which was still in dry dock, Chief Biro was assigned guard duty.

Heroic adventures soon followed. USS *Stewart*, with assistance from USS *Edsall*, saved a burning oil tanker and rescued survivors at great risk to themselves, earning national recognition.

Chief Biro's family believed he'd shared a cabin, but as a chief (I learned from Chief Mac during several Work Weeks), I believed he bunked in the "goat-locker" forward. The area was being restored and not open to the public until the following year.

With solemn promises to be careful, I took Chief Biro's adult kids down one level to the goat-locker where 12 chiefs slept, ate, and hung out. The bright stainless-steel refrigerator, restored by Texas A&M-Galveston cadets, is still there. Forward were the heads.

Daughter-in-law Mary videoed, while son, Rich, asked me questions.

Topside, the video brought a deep 75-year-old-memory-lit smile to the Chief's eyes. That made the work that volunteers from all over the county did on *Stewart* worth it. A small reward for a remarkable man and those who gave so much.

After World War II Chief Biro continued to serve—he was a D.C. police lieutenant for 26 years. He went on to work with Richard Paugh, his best buddy from his service aboard USS *Stewart* and a manager at NCR Corporation.

With Spencer Ernst, another volunteer and veteran, we climbed down carrying Chief Biro's walker. Chief Biro descended the ladders of his youth one more time, still a strong self-assured independent man of the sea.

Note: Chief Rudy Biro just celebrated his 98th birthday, still going strong, as this went to press. The Biro family has greatly supported the Galveston Naval Museum through the Edsall Class Veteran's Association. His son Rich and I are pen pals, when we aren't down in the bilges painting.

USS Stewart to the Rescue
Sallee

Date: 9 April, 1945. Tonight, for once, the seas were calm—for the North Atlantic, rough seas anywhere else. Still, it was possible to spot the flame 20 miles out. The captain, Lt. Cmdr. Alvin Chesley Wilson Jr., U.S. Naval Reserve, hailed from Tennessee. To get a better look, he stepped up onto the pulpit and leaned over the cold steel, focusing his glasses–binoculars–on the yellow spot ahead.

A blast of ocean spray clouded his view as *Stewart's* sharp bow blasted through the waves. Even though the flying bridge provided the best unobstructed view from which the captain could operate a destroyer escort (DE), it was exposed to the elements.

Shouting over the wind he yelled at the seaman, "All ahead full." Cupping his hands over the bronze tube the seaman yelled down "All ahead full." Squeezing 22 knots out of a destroyer escort was out of character.

The ship was built to "shepherd" slow convoys to England, and to hunt slow, submerged Nazi U-boats. This was World War II.

As the flames grew larger on the horizon, it became clear to the crew that *Stewart's* role today would be that of a fireboat. Capt. Wilson also believed they would be close to the heat. He ordered all ammunition moved from the portside of the ship to the starboard.

Doc was notified. *Stewart* carried an M.D. only because he served eight other DE's when needed. Doctor or patient were transferred between ships by a bosun's chair while underway. A dangerous thrill ride. He taught Chief Biro how to play chess.

The was no machine aboard a DE to move ammo, only sailors. No conveyor belts, cranes or elevators, just muscles and sweat. As chief gunners mate, Rudy Biro, a plank-owner on *Stewart* recalled, everything—150 depth charges, each weighing over 300lbs, and hundreds of 13lb. 3-inch shells—had to be moved to the starboard side. This was one reason DE's carried a large crew; it was human horsepower. The other was to still be able to sail the ship if half of the crew were killed in action.

Almost an hour later came the command "All stop," as Capt. Wilson solved a complex formula—windage, current, speed, waves, and turns, as he gently brought *Stewart* parallel with the midsize tanker.

Flames burned from stem to stern. The tanker, SS *Saint Mihiel*, had been rammed midship by another U.S. tanker, SS *Nashbulk*.

Carrying an eight-million-gallon capacity load of high octane aviation fuel, SS *Saint Mihiel* was a ticking time bomb.

Saint Mihiel's senior surviving deck officer, Second Mate Bruno Bernard Baretich, had given the order to abandon ship almost immediately. Upon collision, some men had been knocked off the ship. Thirty-two never made it, dying in the flames or from the fumes.

There had been no time to load the lifeboats, so 23 men jumped into the frigid waters in their life jackets. Fifteen were retrieved by *Stewart*, the rest were rescued by four other DE's when they arrived on scene.

As *Stewart* approached within 20 feet, the crew had every firehose available shooting full blast into the fire. No one was left aboard *Saint Mihiel*.

The *Stewart*, with 220 men, was at risk too. As firehoses continued to spray across the narrow gap between the ships, the heat blistered *Stewart's* haze gray hull paint. Those sailors without fire suits had buckets of water dumped over them by other crew members as the hot air between the vessels gushed against them.

The fire burned all along the tanker, and even though the *Stewart's* explosive-filled magazines had been redistributed, they, regretfully, had to ease away.

Pre-dawn revealed SS *Mihiel* still intact but still burning. She had remained ablaze throughout the night. The decision was made to attempt to salvage her.

Again, *Stewart* approached along portside as the crew beat down the flames with fire hoses until some of *Stewart's* crew, along with Second Mate Baretich and 14 *Mihiel* volunteers, were able to jump back on the SS *Saint Mihiel*.

From *Stewart*, they brought chemical foam apparatuses and every portable piece of firefighting equipment that was on board, such as the P-250 "Handy Billy" pumps. Eventually, by cooling the decks, they forced the flames back over the open hatches. This killed the fire at its source. The *Stewart* crewmembers and *Mihiel's* Merchant Mariners had "stood in constant danger of becoming surrounded and trapped."[1]

"Canvas hose lines smoldered as they lay on the hot decks. Constantly present in the minds of the men who had volunteered to come aboard the abandoned tanker was the thought that an explosion might occur. The *Stewart* did not stay alongside because she could not expose her own explosive filled magazines to the consuming heat for long."

USS *Edsall*, the namesake for this class of destroyer escorts, arrived on site to relieve *Stewart*. Begrimed, *Stewart's* exhausted crewmembers reboarded their ship. The remainder of the SS *Saint Mihiel* crew stayed aboard while "USS *Edsall* safely brought the battered slow moving SS *Saint Mihiel* through the fog shrouded, crowded channel leading to a safe anchorage in New York."[2]

USS *Stewart* meanwhile escorted the other tanker, SS *Nashbulk*, back to New York to the Brooklyn Naval Yard, according to Chief Biro.

A press release from the Secretary of the Navy dated July 6, 1945 was titled, "Heroic Actions Saves Tanker After Collision Off East Coast." The release detailed the actions of the Stewart crew and officers.

The Presidential Merchant Marine Distinguished Service Medal was awarded to Second Mate Baretich, citing "His extraordinary courage and skillful seamanship under circumstances which indicated possible annihilation will be a lasting inspiration to all seamen of the United States Merchant Mariners."

Through these men's actions," it continued, "the fires were brought under control, engines turned over, and by utilizing the after-emergency steering gear, and stationing himself in the bow—the bridge having been completely gutted—the SS *Saint Mihiel* was successfully brought to New York. The still smoldering fires were extinguished, valuable cargo salvaged and the vessel repaired."

As I finished telling this story to a veteran Merchant Mariner, who transported munitions to Desert Storm, he commented, "That was a heck of a job of seamanship!"

Today you can walk the decks of USS *Stewart* and touch her hull, where 75 years ago, the flames heated the thin steel. And you can reflect on the courage displayed by Chief Rudy Biro and the other crew members.

Another connection is that the Edsall Class Veteran's Association holds two work weeks on *Stewart* each year. Come to the Galveston Naval Museum and live history. Chief Biro might even show up.

1,2: From Secretary of the Navy press release dated July 6, 1945.

```
                        SECRETARY OF THE NAVY
                     OFFICE OF PUBLIC RELATIONS
                          Washington 25, D.C.

HOLD FOR RELEASE
PRESS AND RADIO
UNTIL 9:00 A.M. (E.W.T.)
JULY 6, 1945

     HEROIC ACTION SAVES TANKER AFTER COLLISION OFF EAST COAST

        The tanker SS ST. MIHIEL is afloat today, ready once again to carry her
vital gasoline supply to distant battle zones, because of the recent heroic ef-
fort of two destroyer escorts of the Atlantic Fleet, the USS STEWART and the
USS EDSALL.

        Rammed by another tanker, the SS NASHBUCK, with whom she was in convoy, a
few hundred miles off the East Coast, on the afternoon of last April 10, the ST.
MIHIEL was damaged amidships and instantly set aflame from bow to stern.  Six
million gallons of high octane gasoline provided fuel for the raging inferno.

        Deadly fumes swept beneath the heat of the flames and drove the crew to
the rail.  Thirty-two of these men died before reaching the safety of liferafts
and boats.  Others, too badly burned and exhausted to swim, were kept alive only
by the life jackets which had been thrown over the side.

        Four other destroyer escorts, the USS RHODES, USS BRISTER, U.S SELLSTROM
and the USS RICHEY, helped to rescue survivors from the ST. MIHIEL.

        The tanker was unmanned and ablaze from stem to stern when the first de-
stroyer escort to reach the scene, the USS STEWART, came alongside.  She was under
the command of Lieutenant Commander Alvin Chesley Wilson, Jr., U.S.N.R., whose
father lives at 306 Emariland Boulevard, Knoxville, Tennessee.  Fire-fighting
crews on the STEWART poured streams of water on the blazing ship.  From the port
side they beat down the flames so men could board her with chemical foam appar-
atus and every piece of fire-fighting equipment that was portable aboard.

        By cooling the decks and forcing the flames back over the open hatches
and eventually killing the fire at the source, the Navy crew from the STEWART
stood in constant danger of becoming surrounded and trapped.

        Canvas hose lines smoldered as they lay on the hot decks.  Constantly
present in the minds of the men who had volunteered to come aboard the abandoned
tanker was the thought that an explosion might occur.  The STEWART did not stay
alongside because she could not submit her own explosive-filled magazines to the
consuming heat for long.

        The fire had been brought under control when the USS EDSALL, the destroyer
escort which had come as a relief for the STEWART, arrived.  They relieved the
begrimed, exhausted men from the STEWART, and with the remainder of the ST.
MIHIEL's crew safely brought the battered, slow moving ship through the fog-
shrouded, crowded channel leading to a safe anchorage in New York, while the USS
STEWART escorted the SS NASHBUCK into the harbor.
```

Actual copy of press release telling the story of USS Stewart's heroic action to save the tanker after the collision. Notice it is dated July 6, 1945, three months after the incident, for security reasons.

Chief Petty Officer (ret.) Mac Christy at his work station aboard Stewart during a recent Edsall Class Veteran Association's Work Week. Since 2011, Chief Mac has led a crew which has saved Stewart from a rusty wreck to 85% restoration.

Cooking up a Work Week
Sallee

What would move him to drive straight through from Phoenix to Seawolf Park's Galveston Naval Museum? Well, a Ford pickup, with a stove and huge refrigerator in the back. But what motivated him is a longer, more interesting story.

Mike Morin, retired air traffic controller and Army medic also ran a catering company. See a Navy connection to USS *Stewart* and *Cavalla* yet? No? Keep reading.

Well, back about eight years ago, Chief Mac Christy, a former destroyer escort engineering chief petty officer, continued to lead men (and women) by organizing work weeks to save USS *Stewart* from completely rusting away. As he is known to say, "Rust never Sleeps." Folks of all ilks came from all over the country to lend their expertise, whatever skill level, to restore the ship and submarine.

The orange rust attack was first slowed, then over the years held in check and the past year is in retreat as more of the ship is reclaimed and opened to the public. The rust battle is often in closed areas still off-limits for safety reasons, such as the engine compartments.

Slowly, week by work week there's more to see: the crew's head (bathroom—no privacy there), the captain's cabin, the bridge, the forward 3' gun, officer country and most recently the "goat locker" where the CPOs bunked and hung out. The compartment also houses the first display focused on a plank owner—an original crew member who boarded right here in Galveston in 1943, Chief Rudy Biro. He is still going strong and inspected the ship last year in person.

So why do folks from all over, paint, scrape rust, or fix complex 75-year-old machines?

A large part of the answer is Chief Mac. He recruits well, supervises and encourages people to come back. That is how a recently retired Social Work professor ended up crawling on his stomach in mucky bilge water, scraping rust off the 75-year-old keel. And gladly signing up for the next Work Week.

Certainly, we all have tasks at home, but I even hire painters so I can go work on the ship. No, I am not crazy—by working on the ship I get to eat the best food in the fleet.

Bringing us back to Mike, the cook, and his wife, Susan, the baker. First of all, he is full of life—even at 4 a.m. Okay, make that by 5:30 a.m. They used to live in Kansas, where Susan worked with Virgie, Chief Mac's wife. Chief Mac worked his recruiting magic and soon an Army guy was fixing 400 meals with custom made omelets, 600 cookies, 360 brownies and other snacks, a traditional turkey dinner in November, and fresh seafood dinner in May, for 35 hardworking folks.

My first week of the "best food in the restoration fleet" I moaned that I was going to gain more weight than on a 10-day cruise. Mike said, "No you won't, you'll work it all off." You know he was right!

Mike's motivational statement, posted each morning above the coffee pot, keeps us thinking as we joke with old and new friends while beating back rust.

See Greyhounds
Sallee

Watch *Greyhound*. Not the dogs in La Marque, but in the North Atlantic in February, 1942. Based on C.S. Forester's, *The Good Shepard*, this is Apple TV's showing of Tom Hanks's gripping movie of naval warfare during WWII.

Filmed on a real-life destroyer, USS *Kidd*, so much action and emotion are packed into the tiny bridge and combat information center (CIC) it's exhausting.

Code named *Greyhound*, the Fletcher class swift ship "herds" 37 tankers and cargo ships in a convoy across the "Pit", the sea where there was no aircraft coverage for a long 50 hours. The supplies would keep England in the war against the Nazis. No cargo, no survival of democratic freedom in England.

On his first command, Tom Hanks's character is a father figure to three hundred 19-year-old sailors while playing a deadly, complex match with eight enemy U-boats—the wolf pack.

The sailors in the movie represented Galveston's Neal Van Dussen, who joined the Navy at 17, and "did his job" on a destroyer escort. Neal was recognized during the last Veteran's Day Ceremony at Seawolf Park where his story was told by Mayor Craig Brown.

Watching the movie, you feel—like Neal did for real—the cold spray, smell the smoke, hear the screaming, feel the ship's never-ending motion. You are touched by the sailors' faces with Academy Award winning emotions, fear, courage, and thrills.

If you were not in the Navy, though, you may wonder what the heck is going on—the jargon is fast and furious: "I have the con." "Target bearing 087 degrees." "Come around to 320 degrees." "Ready K-gun." All this while guns blast and the ship rocks.

Meanwhile, down in the CIC, the executive officer, the XO, draws on a circular table each ship's location while the sonar man listens to propellers, calling out information shown on the primitive radar, which sometimes works.

Greyhound puts on display the deadly underwater warfare which played the critical difference in WWII.

Galveston has the only museum in the world where, side by side, there's a beautifully restored submarine and a destroyer escort, whose mission it was to sink submarines. Docents, many of whom will teach you the jargon as they were sailors themselves, provide an enhanced visitor experience to all ages.

Visitors stand where gun crews manually handled rounds, just like *Stewart* plank owner Chief Rudy Biro explains on a sound box. You stand on the bow and smell the sea. The Country could come together and celebrate *Greyhound* by visiting our memorial.

What a gift the Cavalla Historical Foundation and Edsall Class Veterans Association volunteers have prepared for veterans, their families, school kids and groups who have the sleepover-on-board experience and programs. For a virtual tour and information visit: galvestonnavalmuseum.com.

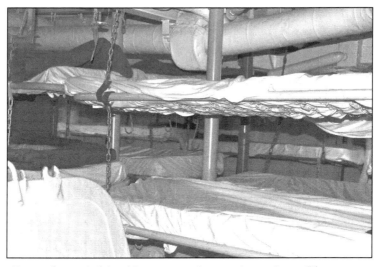

Restored crews' aft berthing space on Stewart, just as it was 75 years ago.

Preamble to Tolling the Boats

Honoring our fallen submarine heroes is fundamental to our creed as members of U.S. Submarine Veterans (USSVI), which is "To perpetuate the memory of our shipmates who gave their lives in pursuit of their duties while serving their country."

In our participation we remember those gallant submariners who made the supreme sacrifice while performing their duties with honor integrity and courage and we demonstrate to our families and to our youth by our deeds that we honor them, we pay tribute to them, we salute them, as should all citizens of our great nation.

The *Tolling the Boats* ceremony was originally established by the U.S. Submarine Veterans of World War II. It is a unique and time-honored memorial service and is in keeping with the finest traditions of the Navy. Custom has established that this ceremony be formal, and it honors the memory of those submariners who lost their lives in the line of duty, and especially those who perished during World War II. In the heart of the ceremony the names of each of the U.S. submarines lost, along with the fate of its crew, are read aloud as a bell is tolled for each in turn.

The tolling of the ship's bell reminds us of the debt of gratitude we owe to both our departed shipmates and to those in active service who silently guard the honor of our country who serving silently under the sea. In many ways, the *Tolling the Boats* ceremony formally reaffirms to serving Navy submarine personnel that their current "deeds and sacrifices" follow in the footsteps of their fellow submariners who preceded them.

We shall never forget the ultimate sacrifice they made so we all, and especially our families and loved ones, enjoy the fruits of freedom.

Our thanks to Bryan Lethcoe, CDR, USN (ret.) for providing this copy of the Tolling of the Boats.

Two Bell Ceremony
Held at the Galveston Naval Museum*

In days past, two bells (*toll two bells here*) marked the end of the routine day aboard a ship. It was time for tattoo, and soon, taps would sound throughout the ship. Certainly, this is a most appropriate time to honor our departed shipmates. Ladies and gentlemen, would you please bow your heads.

The toll of the ships bell reminds us of the reverence we owe our departed shipmates (*toll two bells here*).

To those who guard the honor of our country ... upon the sea ... in the air ... and upon foreign soil (*toll two bells here*).

Let it be a reminder of the faith they confide in us (toll two bells here).

Let us who gather here not forget our obligations, and in silence, breathe a prayer for our absent shipmates (*toll two bells here*).

Let us offer a silent prayer for our departed shipmates (*10 second pause*). This moment of reverence we dedicate to the memory of our shipmates who have gone before us (*toll two bells here*).

(*Taps played slowly from the bow of USS Stewart.*)

God bless America!

* Thanks to Chief Mac Christy for providing this copy of the ceremony

Art Vega, USMC (ret.) plays Taps on bow of USS Stewart after the Two Bell ceremony.

We Were Just Boys
Sallee

"We were just boys doing our jobs. The lieutenant taught us hopscotch and marbles. Later he helped me get my high school diploma."

Sitting in a comfortable bungalow in mid-town Galveston, Second Class Sonarman, Cornelus Irewin Van Dussen, "Neal", is telling a story 76 years old. His memory is crystal clear as he explains his Navy days during World War II.

The son of a hard-working first-generation Dutch father, Neal grew up in Michigan. Out deer hunting one day, his car broke down and his father refused to get him. Neal missed his final exams, thus keeping him from playing basketball, so he joined the Navy at age 17 in December, 1942.

A former Sea Scout, he qualified well and was told he would go to school, but first he was sent to a Naval airport in Brazil to load planes. From there it was the shortest distance to fly to Africa.

After a year, he went to Miami for sonar school. Neal recalls being impressed by the Russian soldiers' perfect marching from their hotel. Next assignment was USS *Samuel S. Miles*, a new Cannon-class destroyer escort, DE 183.

Aboard *Miles*, this farm boy traveled through the Panama Canal and off to all the major battles of the Pacific Theater: Leyte Gulf, Okinawa, Iwo Jima, Caroline Islands, New Guinea. Earning eight battle stars, the ship's mission was to shield aircraft carriers from attacks by Japanese planes and submarines. She excelled at both, shooting down—known as splashing—five planes and sinking I-177, a Japanese submarine, carrying an admiral and over 100 troops.

I-177 from 13 miles out was approaching a U.S. aircraft attack force near the Palau Islands. Listening on sonar, Neal heard the propellers of I-177 under the waves and directed the firing of 24 hedgehogs, small mortar rockets. Splash but nothing else. A second set of hedgehogs shot up in an arc hitting the sea 100 yards out. Silence, then boom. A blast so loud it was heard 13 miles away, knocking out *Miles's* radio. For an hour, the task force feared *Miles* was lost, but only I-177 sank.

Man-handling bombs and running through high seas in a complex vessel was always dangerous. Neal's quick thinking saved a sailor burned by a valve failure. But what still haunts Neal was Suicide Cliff in Saipan, where he witnessed thousands of Japanese civilians, including mothers holding babies, jump from high above the rocky beach to their deaths. Japanese propaganda had broadcast that US soldiers would torture and rape them.

Today, after a successful maritime career and a sailing business, Neal longed to tell his story. A story of boys doing what needed to be done and the costs to keep us free. If you visit the Galveston Naval Museum's real destroyer escort, you might even get to thank a veteran in person.

Neal's Visit, 75 Years Later
Sallee

Yesterday afternoon, 75 years ago came alive. I welcomed World War II Sonarman 2nd Class Neal Van Dussen aboard USS *Stewart*. Neal is a plank owner of the sister ship to the *Stewart*, Destroyer Escort, USS *Samuel S. Miles DE* (183).

For 93, he quickly made it up two decks, to the combat information center (CIC). Moving onto the bridge, he stood with hands on the levers (which we had just repaired), eyes forward looking through the porthole, and told the tale.

During World War II, off Okinawa in the spring of 1945, he heard the order, "Full starboard, back one port." As the telegraph operator, he jerked those levers as required, sending the message down three decks to the engine room.

As the bow quickly turned to port, a Japanese kamikaze plane hit the gun mount only 10 feet in front of him—the gun Neal now stared at. The propeller decapitated one sailor before the plane drove all the way into the engine room, injuring 30 more sailors.

"I remember his name was Robert Allen," Neal whispered.

Neal had dived under the table to his left. When he got up, the sailor on starboard watch, just outside the bridge, was covered in blood. He told Neal, "Someone is bleeding all over."

Neal responded, "Check your ear."

For a minute or so, I stood silently with Neal. With his hands still on the handles he said, "It still makes me a bit emotional."

That could be said for all of us. Later, on the way back down to the main deck, we met families whose parents wanted a photo with Neal once they heard his story.

This is why I am honored to scrape rust and stand in the humid heat telling visitors about the men and ships we work on.

Neal has told me several times that officers get too much credit. "Yes, officers are necessary, but seamen do the work."

I asked him what he thought of chief petty officers—CPOs.

"Oh, they're the backbone of the Navy," he said, and went on and on praising CPOs.

So I asked, "Want to see the goat locker?"

Neal's eyes smiled. "Yes, I do."

As an enlisted man on a destroyer escort, he would not have been allowed forward to where the chiefs lived. We entered the space. Neal sat down and studied the displays.

I told him the story of CPO Rudy Biro, a *Stewart* plank-owner, and that those were his whites and greens—uniforms—from WWII. We discussed the many roles USS *Stewart* played in the war.

Then I read the citation for CPO Mac Christy, which is hung next to his dress blues uniform. After I finished reading, Neal said, "Please thank Chief Mac for his service and the work he has led to restore this ship." Squinting, he then asked, "How many stripes does Chief Mac's uniform sleeve have on it?"

Even with Aggie math I was able to count all of them. "Five, times five equals 25 years, right"?

Neal commented, "He must have behaved."

Guess the cutting up came later, I thought to myself.

As we drove to Neal's home, he was quiet, reflective.

Note: 2nd Class Sonarman Neal Van Dussen visited USS Stewart 16 July, 2019.

Above: Sonarman Neal Van Dussen stands with hands on the telegraph, just as he did 75 years ago on the DE USS Samuel S. Miles, when a kamikaze plane crashed through the gun 10 feet in front of him.
Right: Cornelus Irewin Van Dussen, "Neal" at age 17.
(Used with permission.)

A letter arrived this morning from Marie, Neal's wife, a wonderful woman whose mother was a hero in her own right in the French Resistance during WWII.

Marie's letter read:

Dear Alvin,

Thank you for your visit and attention paid to Neal, you make him feel a taste for life again, that is wonderful.

Neal wants to thank you a lot for your commentary in the Daily News; we did not expect it so soon.

You made Neal the hero today at the Senior Day Care "Libbie's Place" where a lady reads the newspapers for all the customers.

My granddaughter, 13 years old, recently came to Galveston for five days. She enjoyed visiting the Naval Museum with me and said that both the destroyer and the submarine gave her a lot to think about the men living aboard and a war situation at sea.

A real great thank you again, and, as you know, you are very welcome anytime."

Signed,

Marie

And indeed, I have been welcomed for many wonderful afternoons. Marie's ice tea is the best, too.

USS Stewart World War II Photos
Sallee

On the following pages are photos which are just now being presented to the general public.

Chief Gunner's Mate Rudy Biro came aboard the destroyer escort, USS *Stewart* the first day it went to sea, remaining part of the active crew until the end of the war. After receiving word that Japan had unconditionally surrendered, "*Stewart* made a perfect 180-degree U-turn." according to CGM Biro.

With the convoy, *Stewart* headed back to Pearl Harbor. After loading aboard war-weary Marines, *Stewart*, *Edsall* and other DE's departed for San Diego and eventually back to Philadelphia. They were finally home.

As the executive officer walked down the gangway, he looked up at CGM Rudy Biro at the rail, smiled, and pitched up several rolls of camera film. The exec. yelled up, "Chief, you will know what to do with these. Good luck!" he added, as he snapped a smart salute, and with that he was off down the pier.

Chief Biro looked at the small black metal rolls and pondered what to do. He knew it was against Naval regulations to take personal photos on ships during wartime. Is that what the exec. meant when he said "You will know what to do with these?"

Well, after all, like the rest of the officers, the exec. was a Navy reservist, as DEs were designed for non-career crews to be able to man them. An Annapolis Academy grad—regular Navy—probably would not have bent the rules.

The chief decided to pay the $160 to develop the rolls of black and white film, and now has graciously allowed us to publish some of those photos.

They provide a glimpse of life on a DE transiting the north Atlantic back and forth, usually at eight to ten knots, with rushes to stations at the sounds of an enemy submarine once in a while. Also shown are other assignments, such as coming to the rescue of an oil tanker on fire, towing ships and routine drills. And the faces of the young crew.

Thanks go out to Chief Biro's son, Rich, for converting the photos to a thumb drive and assisting with the captions. Thanks to Joan Sallee for editing them into focus. And to Mari Anderson for arranging them for print.

These photos are truly priceless.

Ready for action, USS Stewart training off Cuba before beginning North Atlantic convoy duty. Notice "pulpit" upper left side with officer peering down.

Stewart crew in New York City area readies ramp to on-load depth charges off a railroad car on April 12, 1945, just before the death of FDR was announced.

Stewart crew carefully lowers a depth charge through the aft hatch down through the crews' berthing space to the bilge for storage.

*Aft 3' gun crew takes a break during training drills
in Caribbean before heading north.*

*Hand-drawn line points out Chief Biro helping his crew bring
depth charges on board USS Stewart.*

Chief Gunners Mate Rudy Biro helps direct refueling procedure while underway.
Note black fuel line rigged between the ships.

Stewart crew standing along port side midship during refueling.
Today at the Galveston Naval Museum you can walk this same deck.

*Stewart's doctor had injured sailor transferred from tanker
while underway to provide medical attention.*

*Tanker plows through the sea alongside Stewart. Convoys usually could only
make 8-10 knots on the crossing, thus making them easy targets for U-boats.*

Stewart officers inspect tow line running through the bow "bull nose" before being towed by another DE. The Stewart's engines were down.

Stewart crew members move aft on port side taking up slack in line. Note DE beginning to take position for tow.

Stewart approaches SS Mihiel, a tanker, under command of
Captain Alvin Wilson, USNR. Stewart's crew was recognized for heroic action.

USS Stewart, next to the dock with another DE outboard in Brooklyn Naval Yard
being prepared to move to the Pacific theater.

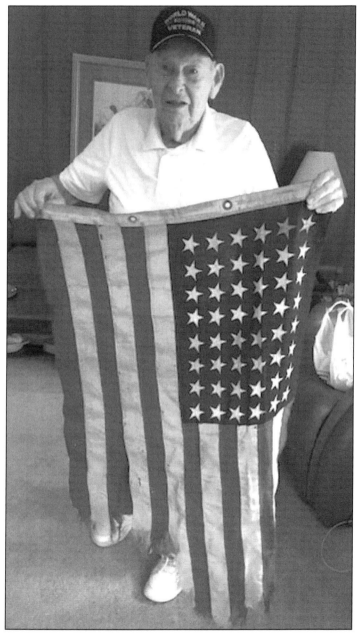

Gunners Chief Rudy Biro at age 97, still going strong, holding the USS Stewart's flag from 1945, which he donated to the Galveston Naval Museum.

CHAPTER 7
Submariners, Seabees & Marines

In This Chapter
Sallee

We continue the sea stories of WWII, this time under the sea, aboard submarines. We begin with the famous "Lucky Lady" USS *Cavalla*. She still serves our country as a living museum in Seawolf Park at the Galveston Naval Museum.

A USS *Cavalla* plank owner, Captain "Zeke" Zellmer's family contributed personal stories and photos of USS *Cavalla's* patrols, including the historic sinking of a Japanese aircraft carrier, which helped turn the War in the South Pacific. "Zeke's" son, John Zellmer, is publishing a book on all the details

Other stories are told through Capt. Wallace A. Greene, as well as the scuttlebutt of a Seabee, a Marine, and even an Army guy.

Ah-OOG-ah! ah-OOG-ah! Dive! Dive!

USS Cavalla today, port side looking forward.

Lucky Lady's Birthday, 29 February
Sallee

"Lucky Lady," World War II slang and humor for a long sweaty stinking steel tube effective killing machine: a submarine. USS *Cavalla* (SS244) commissioned on February 29, 1944, earned the nickname first by the date, a leap year, and then through her combat service record in the South Pacific.

Home to 54 sailors and six officers, who operated a complex football field-long contraption with six forward and four aft torpedo tubes, diesel engines for surface sailing and tons of batteries for underwater propulsion.

Almost 75 years later, I unlocked the hatch and slowly climbed up the narrow twisting ladder to the *Cavalla* conning tower. "Come on up," I yelled down.

John Zellmer, a wiry, gray-haired, recently-retired special education teacher, quickly appeared next to me, a smile of satisfaction as he absorbed the cramped quarters. "Amazing, during an attack there were up to 12 men in here." Moving to the back he added, "I think this is where Dad stood to plot the shot."

His dad, Capt. Zeke Zellmer, a Naval Academy graduate and a plank owner—that's an original officer—visited Cavalla last year to help direct a re-enactment of the attack. Capt. Zellmer was interred with full military honors Arlington National Cemetery, 15 January, 2019.

During the first patrol, on 19 June 1944, *Cavalla* quickly fired a spread of six torpedoes, securing three hits which sank the Japanese aircraft carrier, *Shokaku*, whose planes had attacked Pearl Harbor.

In the quiet we stood on the same deck as John's dad had, 75 years before. But his dad and the crew had suffered through 106 depth charges from three destroyers.

John shared the details. "The depth charging following the attack on *Shokaku* lasted about three hours with about 50% of the charges being fairly close. Several of the early destroyer passes and depth-charging caused a serious flooding problem—over 12 tons of water—in the FTR (forward torpedo room), magnifying the crash-diving past safe depths."

John stood with his hands on the small table, his dad's table, as emotions took over. War continues to impact families even years later. I respectfully retreated.

Life aboard the "Lucky Lady", as with most WWII subs, was difficult service, physically and mentally. Every sailor trained constantly, needing to know all of the complex tasks in case that person was injured. Ten-second showers (if any) and close quarters stunk up the small space. Hot bunking meant no bed to yourself.

Loud diesel engines and the smell of fuel, not to mention being knocked about as pipes leaked during depth-charging, added to the emotional stress. Then there was the fact that proportionally more submariners died in combat than any other service.

And the war sometimes got personal, face to face. John told me a story from the log.

In the ranks of plank owners was outgoing Korean-American Yon Ho Kim, an electrics mate 3rd class. On 18 July, 1944, *Cavalla* sunk a 50-ton sampan in the San Bernardino Strait. Several Japanese seamen were swimming amongst the wreckage. On the surface, Skipper Kossler had Yong Ho Kim EM3c, who spoke a little Japanese, try to entice the survivors to come aboard *Cavalla*. There were no takers. Japanese propaganda won out and the men later drowned, probably, if the sharks didn't get them. That was as personal as it gets.

Today, we are the lucky ones to have USS *Cavalla*, part of the Galveston Naval Museum, which also displays USS *Stewart*, the Memorial Plaza, the sail of USS *Tautog* and USS *Carp's* conning tower. The museum, located at Seawolf Park, is a living exhibit.

Visitors may walk through *Cavalla* and experience the living and work spaces of this war machine. Even children speak softly as if in a sanctuary. Thanks to volunteers' hours of work, this is a site of remembrance and understanding.

We celebrated Cavalla's special birthday on 28 February, 2000, including a VIP tour with Chief Garcia at 1300 hours (1:00 p.m.) followed by birthday cake—I had seconds.

Lcdr. H.J. Kossler cuts the cake at Cavalla's commissioning party. Crew members and significant others look on, all with brave smiles, before shipping out.

Cavalla's Wayward Torpedo

As told by Capt. "Zeke" Zellmer. Recorded by John Zellmer.
(Used with permission)

On the morning of March 23, 1944, we began taking exercise torpedoes aboard the USS *Cavalla*. Torpedoes one and two were lowered into the forward torpedo room (FTR) and moved to the racks before checking. As the third torpedo was positioned in the rack it was rolled over to begin its check. While a torpedo is outside of the tube, it is kept safe by having a 'keeper' inserted behind the starting lever (trigger); the 'keeper' is kept in place by tying it with a light line.

Murphy's Law intervened and the light line became untied with the 'safety' keeper falling silently to the sailor's bunk below. When the exercise torpedo was moved forward toward the torpedo tube, the starting lever hit a cross piece on the skid and the torpedo motor started! We had a "hot run!"

The propellant in the torpedo—a combustible mix of ethanol and compressed oxygen—ignited, filling the forward torpedo room with a cacophony of noise and billows of smoke. The propellers were spinning fast and there was no stop lever!

As this was happening, I was at my desk in the stateroom just aft of the hatch to that compartment. I got up and stepped out into the passageway to go forward to assist. As I bolted into the passageway, a steward running aft from the FTR (forward torpedo room) bumped me back into my stateroom. As I recovered my balance and started out again, a second steward knocked me back once more! On the third try, I carefully entered the smoky compartment. By now, the noise had abated, but the smoke had not cleared.

The Mark 14 torpedo has a device, called a governor, that shut down the motor before the unabated running could ruin the torpedo. There never was a threat from an explosion of the exercise torpedo, as it did not have explosives in the warhead.

Never again on the USS *Cavalla* was a torpedo rotated on the skids without a thorough check to be certain that the 'keeper' was securely in place!

Note: The Zellmer family donated many of Captain Zellmer's personal items including his uniform. His former cabin has been restored as it was when he bolted out into the passageway and rushed to the forward torpedo room.

Officers assemble on deck of Cavalla just before their first combat patrol. Capt. Kossler is center in t-shirt & shorts, Zeke Zellmer as always in full uniform at right.

From Captain Zeke Zellmer

My dad served in the U.S. Army during World War One. I wanted to follow in his footsteps and took the examinations for entry to the military academies, but there was no opening for the Army. Just one alternate opening for the U.S. Navy. I accepted it.

Luck or fate?

At the Naval Academy, I hoped to prepare to be a pilot, but aircraft training and a queasy stomach suggested otherwise. I chose submarines.

Luck or fate?

Nearing graduation from Annapolis, I chose to commission the fierce sounding submarine, USS *Shark II*. A classmate convinced me to switch boats, so I chose the USS *Cavalla*! On her 3rd war patrol the *Shark II* was lost with all hands.

Luck or fate?

On *Cavalla's* first war patrol our orders were to scout and report the movements of Japanese naval and supporting vessels, not ATTACK! A Japanese tanker refueling convoy and then a Japanese naval convoy steamed past us. Report, don't attack! Frustration! Orders changed—ATTACK, then report! Shortly, a Japanese carrier fleet, with IJN *Shokaku* crossed the periscope hairs. Fire torpedoes, scratch one flattop!

Luck or fate?

Subsequent Japanese anti-submarine depth-charging on us drove the *Cavalla* well below safe diving depth. We survived 106 depth charges.

Luck or fate?

On shore leave in Fremantle/Perth, Australia, I met a woman whose name was mentioned to me by an Annapolis classmate. I fell head over heels in love with Babs Miller after the briefest of courtships.

Luck or fate?

With the war against Japan moving north in late 1944, I was not sure the *Cavalla* would return to Australia! Yes, we were ordered one last time to Australia, so Babs and I were able to be married!

Luck or fate?

The USS *Cavalla* was my home for nearly two years, from commissioning to almost the surrender of Japan in 1945. We, the crew members of our Lucky Lady endured periods of boredom and terror, laughter and tears, but mostly comradeship aboard this living boat, our Lucky Lady!
Sincerely,
Ernie
Lt.(jg) E. J. Zellmer

Note: Captain Zellmer's son, John, drafted the above letter. The Zellmer family continues his proud service through support of the Cavalla Historical Foundation. John even shows up in the bilges to scrape rust. A devoted family for sure. (Used with permission)

Cavalla crew members & significant others celebrate, probably in New London, where the sub was built. Yon Ho Kim EM3c is center back row holding a glass. Photo permission of John Zellmer.

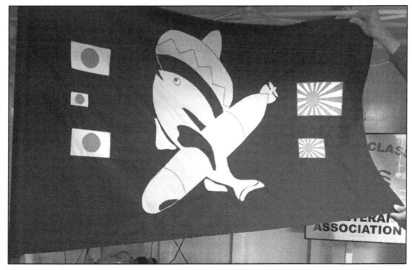

Cavalla battle flag designed by Capt. Zeller depicting the Gulf of Mexico fish, made to look aggressive with the torpedo. Note the smaller flags which list the sinking of Japanese ships. Photo permission of John Zellmer.

How the USS Cavalla Got Here

Excerpted from Bill Cherry's book, *Galveston Memories*, 2000 VanJus Press, Galveston, Texas. (Used with permission.)

The USS *Cavalla* has been a museum to World War II submarine veterans since it was first parked at Seawolf Park's shore edge in 1972. In recent months (1999), officials of the parks board and the U.S. Submarine Veterans of World War II sparred over how to rectify its now dilapidated condition.

Many of us hoped the *Cavalla* would be returned to being a well-kept monument, but not primarily for the reasons you might think. Our wish was for it to remain as the personal legacy of former American National Insurance Co. assistant vice president, James A. Woodall.

Let me describe Woodall for those of you who didn't know him. He was a snappy dresser—new suits, ties, shoes and hats every season from Walter Pye's. He was how actor James Cagney would have looked, walked, talked and acted had the good Lord not had other more important things on his mind the day he created Cagney.

Woodall liked people. People liked Woodall. He began his career in the insurance business as an office boy with Reserve Loan Life in Dallas, advancing through the ranks until he enlisted in the Navy in World War II.

He trained as a member of the ground crew for naval aviation, but shortly thereafter volunteered for submarine duty.

He was aboard the Tender U.S. *Griggin* in the Philippines when the war ended.

Woodall returned to Reserve Loan Life, and was brought to Galveston when the company was bought by American National Insurance (ANICO). W.L. Vogler and R.A. Furbush were running ANICO then.

As time passed, Woodall became the division manager over a number of the company's insurance policy administrative departments. He also married Kay, who was Vogler's executive assistant.

It was in the early 1970s that Woodall decided it was time for him to make his mark. He began to spend countless hours working to convince local and national authorities that a World War II submarine should be bought and made into a museum. That museum should be placed at Galveston's Seawolf Park.

Woodall saw it as a memorial to the many veterans who had been in the submarine service. He saw it as a money-making attraction for Galveston.

Over the following twenty-five years, Woodall's gentle push paid off.

End Note: The museum became the American Undersea Warfare Center which added the destroyer escort USS Stewart a couple of years later. Today, with the USS Tautog sail from the nuclear cold war submarine and the conning tower from USS Carp, plus the two restored vessels are now part of the Galveston Naval Museum, operated by the Cavalla Historical Foundation.

*Taken the year before CHF was
founded to rescue the Cavalla from
the Galveston Park Board.*

*Taken three years after the Cavalla Historical Foundation raised and spent
over two million dollars to restore the Cavalla. Photos courtesy of Cavalla
Historical Foundation. Used with permission.*

168

From Typo to Naval Captain
Sallee

On a warm autumn day in 1935, battleships laid at anchor in the Long Beach Bay. A large flat-bottomed "Liberty" boat approached the wharf, spilling a hundred sailors out, landlubbers for a day. Five 10-year-old boys jumped on for the return trip to the ship. Boarding the USS Pennsylvania, the boys roamed the main deck, like kids do on the USS Texas today. On the return ride, Wally, one of the boys, decided his life goal was to attend the Naval Academy and become an officer.

At age fourteen, in the heart of the Depression, he learned the brutal truth. As the son of an enlisted sailor with no political connections, he hadn't a chance of attending the Academy.

Three years later Pearl Harbor was attacked. Entering at the lowest rank, Wally became a Navy signalman on Merchant Marine ships, which had the highest death rate per capital of any service, except Marines.

Four years and 14 trips across the Pacific later, he saw a notice announcing the V-12 program. This expansion of the Academy, through selected universities, would prepare 100,000 new officers. Wally was first in line for the exam.

Passing the exam opened a big bright door for Wally. Asked which university he wanted to attend, he said, "University of Washington."

The instructor said, "Fine, UW it is."

A few days later, his orders arrived. He was to report to Washburn College in Topeka, Kansas. The typist had made a typo.

Not discouraged, he packed for the heartland, far from the sea. Completing his two semesters and playing on the football team, he was sent with all Washburn Navy grads to the next school. They boarded a train to the University of New Mexico (UNM), on the Rio Grande.

He excelled at UNM, too. Before long, he was announcing football on the radio, engaged to a wonderful girl, and head of the Navy ROTC Midshipmen unit.

Leading the unit running on the track at 5:30 a.m. in July, 1945, half the sky instantly blasted light. No noise or wind, just bright light. It was the first A-bomb test, 130 miles south in the desert.

On graduation day, he led the midshipmen in parade, was best man at one wedding and groom at his own that evening. He attended to every detail, including tapping each bride with the broad side of a sword as she walked under the sword arch.

At 10 a.m. the next day, he and Suzy, his bride, headed out driving to San Francisco for his first assignment on a destroyer as an ensign. A Naval officer at last.

Over the next decades he advanced to the rank of captain. Only one other person has risen from the lowest rank like Captain Wallace A. Greene did. Finishing his story last week, I said, "Uncle Wally, if it hadn't been for that typo, you wouldn't have married Aunt Suzy and we wouldn't be sitting here right now."

"Many small disappointments turned into good fortune in my career," he responded.

That is one typo that I am glad was made.

Just in Time at the Wharf

He arrived at the wharf just in time. No, he was not a late cruise ship passenger. This story begins with a childhood dream of becoming a Naval Officer.

Ensign Wallace (Uncle Wally) A. Greene, was commissioned through the V-12 program during WWII. He entered as a Reserve Officer. Following WWII and three years aboard destroyers he wanted to be regular Navy.

The quickest path in 1949 was to get his Dolphins—the pins awarded to qualified submarine officers. Soon, with Aunt Suzy, he was off to New London, Connecticut, for sub school. Graduating, he was given orders to report to the USS *Remora* (487), in Japan. He had seven days to drive across the country before reporting in San Francisco.

He and Aunt Suzy set off at a leisurely pace. Every morning he dialed in CBS news. Four days into the trip, CBS announced the invasion of South Korea by the North. He drove straight to San Francisco.

Walking into the Naval Personnel Office, he stated his name. The personnel officer said, "We've been waiting for you, Mr. Greene. You're needed in Japan ASAP. Be at the bus stop in thirty minutes. You are going on the *Boxer*." He was a bit puzzled. If he was wanted in Japan so quickly, why was the Navy was putting him on an aircraft carrier, not a plane?

Arriving at the dock an hour later, he rushed aboard as the lines were let loose. The carrier was packed with P-51 fighter airplanes. Even the elevators had planes on them.

Setting sail at thirty-two knots (most cruise ships go about twenty-two knots) the *Boxer* raced to Japan on the great circle course, following the curve of the Earth. The planes were desperately needed in Korea.

With a record crossing, *Boxer* pulled into Yokosuka, faster than flying island to the island. Wally and ten other submariners were the first ushered off. A Jeep and truck were waiting. The Jeep driver yelled, "Who's Greene? Get in." Off at breakneck speed, they pulled up to a submarine nest, where six subs were tied-up side to side.

The middle sub was getting underway. Uncle Wally saw a large 487 on the sail. He didn't need to be told to run. As he boarded the *Remora*, the captain said, "You are junior officer of the watch." Wally was handed binoculars as he passed his sea bag to a sailor.

An hour later, clear of the harbor, the captain ordered, "Mr. Greene, take us down to 280 feet." His first official dive. Eight other officers piled into the small control room (like the *Cavalla's*) to watch the new guy mess up. Thanks to a cold thermal layer, he was able to level off just right, even at two knots, much to the disappointment of his new fellow officers.

The captain was impressed with Uncle Wally. As was the Navy with his service, which later included command of the *Albacore*, the first sub with a curved bow.

Being early paid off. Maybe that's where I got it.

On Eternal Patrol

Captain Wallace A. Greene, Uncle Wally, advanced through the ranks, having gone from the lowest rank, sailor, to the rank of captain, with increasingly more critical commands. He was a Mustang who actually followed Navy regulations better than some Annapolis grads did. Admiral Rickover comes to mind …

When my family and I visited Portsmouth the summer of 1960, Uncle Wally commanded the experimental submarine, *Albacore*. The sub was just a big tube. I ventured it looked like a large drain pipe. He said, "You're right, but it's getting a new bow and stern." And it did, the first of each, which are now on every U.S. sub.

The next April, we got word that a Portsmouth-based sub was missing. We held our breath for what seemed like forever until we found out it was the new *Thresher* (SSN 593), not the *Albacore*.

Then I felt guilt. *Thresher* remains on eternal patrol.

In the late 1960s, Uncle Wally became a squadron commander of six nuclear advanced boats in Norfolk. One of them was the USS *Scorpion* (SSN 589). On 22 May, 1968, *Scorpion* was the last US submarine to be lost to date.

As a college freshman, my family and I visited the Greene's for Christmas, 1968. We had a wonderful dinner in the officer's mess aboard the USS *Onion*, the squadron's tender. All the shrimp I could eat.

After dinner Uncle Wally took us through *Scorpion's* sister ship, the SSN *Sculpin*. I sat at the helm and was amazed at how large the interior was compared to the WWII subs I had toured. Contemplating being in this space for six months straight, though, it began to shrink.

Later my dad, a retired commander, USNR, told me *Scorpion* sank after leaving Spain and that Uncle Wally hadn't even seen it for six months. I never asked Uncle Wally about it, even after he began to share stories of his life with me.

Even as a civilian, the Tolling of the Boats brings enormous emotions, and a bit of understanding of the meaning of being on eternal patrol.

From Ken Greene, Uncle Wally's son: "You shouldn't have mentioned Adm. Rickover, 'cause any nuc officer that had to be interviewed by him has lots of stories, most of them true and not greatly embellished! My senior year at Naval Academy I went to an interview with the admiral. After I went, Dad told me that he, in the early 1960s, went for an interview with then Capt Rickover. Dad wasn't selected for the nuclear program and he remembers saying to himself at the time that he'd outlast that old scrawny SOB and make a career outside of the nucs. After I went and saw the adm., Dad said it turns out he'd never been so wrong, not only did the old SOB outlast Dad but then his own son had to go be interviewed by him as well!"

This is what it looked like when Cavalla's Captain Kossler & crew lined up the shots which sank the Japanese aircraft carrier. Uncle Wally leveled the boat in a space such as this. Photo permission of John Zellmer.

Uncle Wally and the Albacore
Sallee

Uncle Wally would never talk about his Navy days when I visited. In graduate school at Arizona State University, I somehow ended up on the national board of the National Association of Social Workers, a 150,000-strong organization headquartered in Washington D. C.

I would fly in a few days early so I could see the sites, including the Watergate hearings, John Sirica's federal court, and the Capitol. Aunt Suzy would drive me into D.C. each morning. One very rainy day, she took me to Mount Vernon while she waited in the car. I was the only tourist that day, so I got a special behind the scenes tour.

Each evening I was in town, Uncle Wally and I would go down to the basement to watch sports. He was a big fan, especially football. I would try to engage him in a conversation about the Navy, but that was a closed topic. The only exception to his silence was during the war between Israel and Egypt. At that time, he worked at Crystal City (spy's-ville) in Naval Intelligence. He said only that at least we saw how our offensive and defensive weapons worked against each other.

Years later, on a Big Band-themed cruise in 2010, we visited Key West, where he had captained the USS *Triante*. Standing on the highest deck forward, he gripped the rail until his knuckles turned white.

"That man didn't toss that line right!"

I replied, "Uncle Wally, this isn't a Naval ship, just a flag of convenience passenger cruise ship."

That opened the door, and he showed me where the sub pen was on the south side. Then later, in Truman's Little White House, where he used to go to meetings.

Leaving Key West, we passed by an island where the *Triante* practiced putting Gurkhas from Nepal ashore in a raft and retrieving them in preparation of a potential invasion of Cuba.

My last visit with Uncle Wally was at my cousin Trish's home, for Aunt Suzy's birthday. He and I spent days in the den where he detailed his love and life in the Navy.

But one story didn't quite jibe.

In the book, U.S.S. *Albacore: Forerunner of the Future*, by Robert P. Largess and James L. Mandelblatt, I found two paragraphs on page 127:

"Howell Russell and New Hampshire State Representative John McCarthy remember *Albacore's* sixth commanding officer Lt. Cmdr. Wallace A. Greene with particular affection. During his command 569 (*Albacore*) seems to have acquired her only service nickname. "The crew used to call her 'Wally and His Little Red Wagon' says McCarthy. "He was an ex-enlisted man, a first-class signal man. He rose from the ranks and made captain before he retired—he was division commander of submarine squadron 6 in Norfolk when the *Scorpion* went down.

"He was a big man. When we were going to Bermuda, Wally would say to Bob McConnell—one of the other two men aboard over 6 feet, 'bring an extra set of whites.' He had a habit of going ashore the first evening dressed as an enlisted man. He'd go to one of the clubs smoking a big cigar. And he'd say, 'The first SOB who calls me captain or says sir, I'll deck him!' He just wanted to be his old self and play sailor for one night."

I knew and wrote about how Uncle Wally made 14 voyages across the Pacific on merchant ships as a Naval signalman during World War II. When the V-12 program (an extension of the Naval Academy to universities across the country) began, he was the first to sign up. A typo ordered him to Washburn University rather than the University of Washington, for which he'd been approved. After one year, including playing tight end on the football team, he was transferred to the University of New Mexico (UNM), where one August morning at 0500, running around the track he witnessed the first nuclear bomb blast. He married Aunt Suzy the day of his commissioning.

All UNM newly-commissioned officers were assigned to destroyers—DD's—"tin cans". When Uncle Wally heard a few years later that submariners were promoted quicker, he transferred to subs. And sure enough, as a "Mustang" he quickly rose through the ranks and captained the USS *Albacore* and USS *Triante*, during the Cuban Missile Crises, earning an E.

After I read this section of the book to Uncle Wally, he said it didn't happen. A Naval Officer to the end. Yet, he did smoke big cigars ...?

GO NAVY, BEAT ARMY!!

Note from Aunt Suzy: As you know he loved the Navy and serving his country. It really was his life. Even after he retired no matter what his age when there was a problem or conflict involving the U.S. he would draft a letter to the president telling them that he was ready and willing to serve wherever needed.

Endnote: My cousin Trish read drafts of this manuscript to Aunt Suzy who was in isolation in a nursing home. As you can see above, Aunt Suzy provided feedback right up to her last day with us. She peacefully passed as we went to press. Thank you, Aunt Suzy, for all your help for your 95 years; a Navy wife to the end.

Scuttlebutt

By Meredith "Joy" Midert-Sallee (Author Sallee's birth mother who died when he was 5.)

The throbbing of the ships engines was the only sound Lee could hear. He sat on the edge of his bunk and leaned forward to keep from hitting the steel tubing of the bunk above.

Just two more days. Then Frisco, he thought. He glanced around the hold. There were two sailors in dungarees silently playing cards on the bunk opposite him and several others apparently asleep in the surrounding bunks. Nothing to do until chow, Lee thought.

He ran his fingers through his thin gray hair. First, they drive you crazy working day and night and then they stick you on a ship to go home with nothing to do. He dragged a long gray box from under the bunk and opened it. He took out socks, skivvies, dungarees and towels and laid them on the bunk beside him. By damn he wasn't a carpenter for nothing. He removed the false bottom around the box and smiled down at a carbine rifle. He picked it up gently and took off the stock.

The inspectors would never guess his sea chest had a false bottom with a rifle hidden in it. It wasn't that he just wanted a gun—he had hunting guns at home but this was his caribe, his friend. He pulled back the bolt and look down the barrel. He could still hear the commander's briefed orders. "We are going on to Okinawa men, the fighting has stopped there but we are to start building a temporary base."

But the fighting had not been over, and ship repaired units fought beside young red-faced Marines. For those six months, he had lived and dozed with that carbine beside him, then by some miracle he had been ordered home and the collection of firearms had been overlooked.

A voice interrupted his thoughts. "Kissing that thing goodbye, Lee?"

"Hell no, Jim, they'll never find it."

Jim lowered himself on the bunk beside Lee. "Guess you haven't heard the latest scuttlebutt. They're going to x-ray our gear in Frisco," he said.

"X-ray! Where did you hear that?"

"Ole Red got a letter from somebody who put in at Frisco last month, and they x-rayed their gear. Couple of guys who had .45s got court martial. That false bottom box isn't going to do you any good if they use x-ray on our stuff."

"Hell, Red's always blowing ..."

"Maybe, but that little .22 pistol of mine is going to have a quiet burial at sea tonight. I don't want to greet my wife from behind bars." Jim stood up and hoisted himself onto the bunk above Lee. "Guess I'll get a little sack time before chow."

Lee replaced the stock of the gun and put it back into the bottom of the sea chest. Well, there it was! Did a carbine mean so much to you that you would risk disgracing your family? He could remember Geraldine's face when he told her that he was shipping out. She couldn't understand why they were taking men of his age. Suppose he came home to her with a dishonorable discharge and a gun. This story is about x-rays was probably just some damn scuttlebutt, but he couldn't really be sure.

The following evening, he watched as one by one his buddies produced pistols, rifles, and even submachine guns, and threw them overboard. The notice had been posted that day that there would be no firearms taken ashore at San Francisco.

Disobeying any of this order would result in court-martial. Lee went down to his bunk. It hadn't said anything about the x-ray but that was probably just to trap them. He took the rifle and gripped tightly. It was cold blue steel. He walked slowly up the ladder onto the deck. It was like murdering a friend. He leaned his elbows on the lifeline and let the carbine lie in his hands. He stood there looking out at the sea. With a sigh his shoulders dropped, and the carbine slide from his hands.

When they had landed on Treasure Island, Lee contrasted the neat white barracks around town with dirt floor tents and death stenched caves. Civilization and hell.

"Come on get your gear ready for inspection," the shore patrolman yelled. Lee unlatched his sea chest and stood back. The inspector opened the lid and pushed all of the clothes first to one side and then to the other.

"You're okay, Mate. Here's your check slip."

The End

Always a lover of flowers, Joy Sallee about 1946 as a college student and author of numerous short stories based on family members' adventures.

Note: This story is one of several stories I found, typed on onion type paper, 65 years after my mother passed. Joy wrote this in 1947. Lee was my grandfather, her father in law.

Scuttlebutt was based on Lee Sallee's actual experiences. The only thing he told us as kids about his adventure as a World War II Seabee on Okinawa was that he got so mad at the "Japs" for destroying his work every night. They bombed the air strip he had repaired the previous day.

After the war, he went on to be the foreman for Height Construction Company, building hospitals, schools and office buildings in and around Los Angles. All with only an Oklahoma eighth-grade education—his dad wouldn't let him go to high school.

The Cupola on the Old Marine Hospital
Sallee

Some people call him John, actually most people did. I called him Johnnie.

Just two years older, growing up he always took care of me. When I was five my birth mother died suddenly, leaving Dad to care for my brother and me. Each day at 5:00 a.m. Dad took us to Aunt Elva's—Dad's sister and Johnnie's Mother.

After breakfast, Johnnie would take my hand and off we would walk toward each of our respective schools. I, toward Mrs. Leonard's basement pre-school, he to Bandelier Elementary.

He taught me the ways of the world, too. We would go out through the back yard, stopping at the tall wood pile so he could properly groom me. The Brylcreem came out of the wood pile and into our hair, the comb swept our hair back, now shiny, into a duck tail. For that James Dean look, off went our belts, hidden under the logs.

Aunt Elva, of course, put logs on the fire and thus one day we were caught. As I recall, the belts were applied to our backsides.

Dad remarried the next year, yet Johnnie and I remained like brothers.

In high school, Johnnie was like The Fonz from *Happy Days*: good looking, very popular. Sunday night youth groups were where the girls were, like the blonde who was Johnnie's steady.

He was the first designated driver.

179

Off to college for a couple of semesters, then soon he was facing the draft. Coming from a Navy family, instead of being drafted into the Army, he joined the Marines.

As kids, in his neighbors' yards, we dug tunnels and buried large grand piano boxes in the ground with trapdoors.

As a Marine, Johnnie did it for real. At five foot six, a tough guy, he ended up as a tunnel rat in Viet Nam with a flashlight and a .45 pistol, wiggling through the muddy openings. He was qualified as an expert on the firing range and a sniper. As a sergeant, he became a drill instructor at Camp Pendleton.

I wrote him at least once a month, until I couldn't take it, thinking he would be killed without knowing how much I valued him. I wrote Dear John letters. The blonde wrote a real Dear John letter.

He was wounded twice, the last time by a mortar. The field surgeon wanted to amputate his leg. Johnnie said no, and kept it and the pain.

He spent six months at what I thought was the Galveston Marine Hospital, the one with the cupola. At his funeral, I learned he might have been in San Antonio. I also learned that while there were a few Marines in Galveston, the main purpose of the hospital was for Merchant Marines.

On 100% disability, Johnnie taught high school, coached football, had two marriages, retired to fishing in Alaska—a functioning man with PTSD.

We drifted apart as older adults. After talking about our childhood, we didn't have anything else in common. He was very angry at the government, that seemed to be all he would talk about. I called each December 6 to wish him Happy Birthday, but that was about it.

For ten years, every time I looked at the cupola on the old hospital, I did think of my Marine cousin Johnnie. Now I know he probably wasn't there, but it is the thought that counts, and for that I am ever grateful to the cupola.

On Thanksgiving Day in 2017, Johnnie died of heart failure, a young 70. He was laid to rest with all military honors at the National Cemetery in Santa Fe, NM, along with so many things I wish I'd told him.

Galveston's Frank Incaprera Jr.
Sallee

Anyone who knows Galveston's Frank Incaprera, knows he has the gift of gab. And if you don't, he'll tell you. It was a gift that served him and gravely wounded soldiers and sailors well during World War II in military hospitals as a U.S. Army corpsman.

Frank Incaprera saw everything, from lost brain—now known as Post Traumatic Stress Disorder—to terrible wounds, to swamp disease. Incaprera worked with injured Marines, soldiers and sailors from mostly the Pacific Theater.

"We didn't have modern drugs or knowledge then, we just tried to keep them comfortable. They were suffering." Incaprera said. "One guy, the driver for a general, had four broken bones in each leg from a Jeep wreck. No pain meds worked. He asked me for whiskey, so I hitchhiked 50 miles to get him a bottle," Incaprera recalls.

Often there wasn't anything even Frank Incaprera could do but visit with the 100 patients assigned to him, freeing up the nurses and doctors to work on other wounded. He wrote letters for them to loved ones, and listened.

"Had the opportunity to work with everything to anything these guys had," he added.

One "opportunity" Incaprera had was to transport, by train, a victim of severe shellshock—mentally ill—from the hospital in Longview, Texas, to Ohio. They were handcuffed together the whole way. Incaprera kept talking. "I didn't know what to do, but I did it," he still remembers.

"I never had any training for this. It was hell, but I was good at it. It was my duty, to do something for my fellow man." Incaprera pauses, "I remember it all very well, and it is still with me."

"One intelligent guy was blinded in combat. He couldn't see a thing. Nothing. He taught me how to play checkers by using letters and numbers." Incaprera spent days playing with him. They advanced to chess.

"The day he was discharged he asked me one more favor. To take him outside and describe in detail everything I saw, the

181

forest, the hospital." To this day, 75 years later, Frank still remembers that moment. "It never leaves." His voice trails off.

One more way Frank brought brightness to their lives was through music. The Incapreras are well known for their long tradition of summer open-air music on the Island. Frank, after duties were completed, played with five other musicians, often accompanying a singer from the USO shows. Two hours of escape from their anguish for the patients.

What we owe veterans can never be repaid. We must honor their service, whether on the front lines of battle or the front lines back home. Frank Incaprera Jr, Galveston's own, is a hero to the hundreds of those he served.

In 2019, we celebrated Veteran's Day at the Galveston Naval Museum at Seawolf Park to honor Frank Incaprera and Neal Van Dussen, recognizing their critical contributions to our country during World War II.

Visit the Galveston Naval Museum on Pelican Island, Seawolf Park, to hear more stories of the Greatest Generation.

CHAPTER 8
Merchant Marine at War

In This Chapter
Sallee

Modern day warfare still demands the sea. In this chapter, author Mike Leahy tells tales of the role of the Merchant Marine during World War II, the sailors of the Merchant Marine suffered more deaths per capita than any other service, except the U.S. Marines. Yet, it took the government until 1988 to recognize them as veterans and even then, only after a lawsuit.

Mike shares his experience from Viet Nam to Desert Storm through the eyes of a seafarer. As détente began to bloom, Mike was there: from the Iron Curtain and Russia's Black Sea, to chewing gum demand, Levi's blue jeans, and even love, back in the USSR, as the song goes. His experiences should be a lesson for the ages, a human story, linked by the convoys of seafarers from all nations.

The sea transit to there and back produced adventures to tell. A pirate in the North Atlantic? And there is the old vodka story, too. How to catch a cab in Odessa (not the Texas city), is not what you would guess. A difficult speech to old enemies went well enough: Mike is still here.

Almost 20 years later, Mike was called to duty again. As part of the U.S. Merchant Marine, he honored his oath of allegiance and went to sea. The first President Bush called on the world and the U.S. military to counter the invasion of Kuwait by Iraqi military forces.

A massive U.S. military build-up began, once again carried out largely by merchant ships sent to the Persian Gulf. Mike provides another personal narrative describing amazing action.

Read about how tons and tons of ammo was carefully stowed away. About how a pallet of 9-millimeter ammunition goes missing. (Is it in the engine room?)

Getting to Ad Dammam makes for a meticulous yarn, too. Passing through the Suez Canal with a ship of ammo is not normal, as Mike explains. All this with the search for a barber on the fantail and a lamb kebob. The end of the cruise back in Savannah, is unlike those experienced after returning from Viet Nam.

For a detailed description of the role the Merchant Marine plays worldwide, come aboard, this is the chapter for you. People, places and ammo, they are all here.

A Cold War Voyage
Leahy

In the early 1970s, the United States entered into a massive, multi-year, grain trade deal with the Union of Soviet Socialist Republics, or USSR. This was ostensibly arranged to moderate our tense relations with the world's other great "Superpower", the Soviet Bear. Many American oil tankers were chartered in those years to carry grain to the Black Sea ports of the Soviet Union, in particular the Soviet Republics of Georgia and the Ukraine, and I soon found myself on a rusty old tanker bound for the Black Sea.

By the time I made my first trip to the USSR, American seamen had already learned that the sale on the Soviet black-market of chewing gum, Levi's blue jeans, and the niceties of Western life that women took for granted such as makeup, feminine hygiene products, and even simple bars of soap would produce a nearly unlimited supply of Russian rubles. Russian currency was valueless outside the borders of the USSR but, since individual Soviets had almost no money at all, a fistful of rubles made a seaman extremely popular when he went ashore and, due to the black-market exchange of chewing gum to rubles, every man was a king.

Unlike the process of loading bulk grain in tankers, which was relatively quick, the discharge process in the Soviet ports was a very slow and often interrupted operation for a myriad of reasons. All in all, it was not uncommon for seamen to be in the Soviet ports for a couple of months, especially if they were discharging at more than one port, as my ship was.

And then there were the long delays caused by the presence of weevils in the grain. When the grain ships arrived in port, the Russian officials inspected the grain and often it was found to contain weevils. This necessitated another couple of week's delay as fumigation pipes were inserted down into the grain in the cargo tanks and some sort of toxic Soviet insecticide was blown into the grain.

During fumigation, the entire complement of officers and crew had to leave the ship and move into a hotel ashore. Only the ship's engineers travelled back and forth to the ship from the hotel to keep the plant on the line. Mariners got an extended and in-depth exposure to regular folks who lived and worked in these ports and an education on what life was really like for the average Soviet citizen that probably no other Westerners had an opportunity to experience.

We soon discovered that, unlike the propaganda with which we had been raised, these people were just like ourselves and everyone else in the world, for that matter. Some were great people, others were jerks, and very few wasted any of their time thinking about the geopolitical world of the two great post-war rivals: the "Superpowers".

However, one thing we had long been led to believe about the average folks of the USSR was true enough, they had very, very, little of most anything, and their day-to-day lives were void of nearly all of the consumer goods and conveniences that we in 1970s America took pretty much for granted. And their housing situations were overcrowded and generally awful. Compared to the West, they lived survival-level lifestyles under the Socialist system. Everyone had just barely the minimum to survive but very few had much more than that. One can only presume that life was far worse for the average man and woman under the czars because there was very little complaining about things.

We loaded our cargo of grain at the old Good Pasture grain elevator in Houston and were scheduled to discharge it in three Black Sea ports: Odessa, Novorossiysk, and Poti. First, of course, we would have to successfully depart Houston.

This voyage was delayed by some four days when a combination of excessive alcohol and general stupidity led our ship to run aground in the Bolivar Roads while attempting to turn the ship around, having inadvertently headed back inbound after dropping off the local pilot instead of heading out to sea. No ships could pass in or out of the three ports of Galveston, Texas City, and Houston, served by the ship channel in the Bolivar Roads until our ship had been freed from the grip of the seabed. Finally departing the Galveston Bar, our voyage began in earnest. Out through the Straits of Florida, we proceeded to Gibraltar and the Pillars of Hercules for bunkering.

By the time we reached Gibraltar (aka Gib), the officers and crew had already made major inroads into the slop chest supply of beer and liquor. Our chief steward knew that we would be in the USSR for an extended but unknown period of time and that the supply of such beverages was unreliable there.

Russian beer is utterly undrinkable and the only liquor available was vodka and something the Russians called cognac but no Frenchman would ever use that term to describe it. Therefore, our local steamship agents in Gibraltar had been instructed to send out by launch several pallets of St. Pauli Girl and Oranjeboom beers, as well as several pallets of assorted hard liquor.

Thus, fortified with both fuel for the boilers and for the crew, we proceeded onward through the Mediterranean (we just call it the Med), up through the Greek Islands of the Aegean Sea, through the Dardanelles to Istanbul, and finally passing through the Bosporus into the Black Sea. Due to the usual delays at the Soviet ports, we sat out at anchor off Odessa for several weeks and were more than ready for a trip down the gangway when at last we reached the wharves.

On that first trip ashore in Odessa, I had the good fortune to be in the company of a few of my shipmates, notably the first engineer, who had already made several trips there and knew the ropes, so to speak. The first lesson was in how to get a ride to the Odessa Seaman's Club when there are no taxis to be seen and you speak no Russian.

We walked up about two city blocks from the dock area to a large avenue and the 1st held a one-ruble bill up in the air. Immediately, a car stopped and picked us up, ready to take us anywhere. With the facility in communication all seamen develop from being in many places where we do not speak the language, we had no difficulty letting the driver know we wanted to go to the Seaman's Club and, in short order, he dropped us off there.

How chewing gum came to be the hottest commodity in the USSR is unclear but appears to have started when the first few American ships arrived and chewing gum was offered to the shoreside personnel and State officials as a courtesy. Little pleasures in life like chewing gum simply did not exist in the dull life of the Soviet citizen, and it soon became the most popular item in the whole Soviet Union.

Since that first ship had Chicklets brand gum, all chewing gum became forever called "Chicklets" by the Russians, but they soon learned that they preferred Wrigley's, Juicy Fruit, and Doublemint, nonetheless referring to all these brands as "Chicklets".

Our chief steward was a particularly enterprising fellow who had ensured that our slop chest contained massive amounts of chewing gum, blue jeans, women's makeup products and tampons. The official exchange rate was only 80 kopecs (less than one ruble) to one dollar but the chewing gum exchange was between five and six rubles to one dollar, and in this manner, we all went ashore as rich men.

That first evening at the seaman's club in Odessa was a revelation. It was a beautiful old building of a Victorian-like design and was clearly built prior to the Soviet-era of buildings in the form of characterless boxes. The interior was all lovely wood paneling and, most importantly to us, it had an actual bar. Bars and pubs, as we know them in the rest of the world, were extremely uncommon in the places I visited on this voyage and so those few places that had them were high on the list of destinations ashore for seamen.

Most local men did their drinking, and an impressive amount of it, at tables in drab, industrial looking restaurants. The next surprise at the Odessa Seaman's Club was the coterie of "ladies of easy virtue" settled in at the bar like a home away from home, which indeed proved to be exactly the case. I learned that, similar to the sub-rosa official encouragement of the black market, this enterprise in a social life for visiting seamen was also arranged behind the scenes by officials. It can be reasonably presumed that this was driven by a desire to give us something to spend all those rubles on. Also, the KGB agents assigned to monitor us every step we took on Soviet soil would have an excuse to spend time with the girls too, ostensibly to afterwards gain from them the major U.S. Government secrets that we would reveal in "pillow talk". Whatever the reasoning, our social life ashore was thus assured.

The Bratislava Restaurant in Odessa was, to my knowledge, the only upscale such place in the city. As such, it was not patronized by most local people for whom a meal there would cost the equivalent of a month's salary. This consideration of course did not apply to our girls. The Bratislava had not only good food, but a musical band. There also could be found an actual sit-down bar, probably the only other one in the city.

We collected the group of girls at the Seaman's Club and proceeded to the Bratislava for a big night. The girls could be relied upon for all arrangements, transport and communications and it fell to my shipmates and I only to order food, beverages, request repeated playing of the only song the band knew in English (a Gershwin tune, I no longer remember which one) and to periodically hand fistfuls of rubles to everyone in sight.

This practice was soon curtailed by the girls, who took over the payment of money to others on our behalf. This no doubt was out of a well-founded concern that we might run out of money before the end of the night and not have any left for the girls themselves next morning.

We had not been dockside in Odessa but a couple of weeks before the officials advised the captain that our cargo orders were changed. The call at Novorossiysk was canceled and we were to sail immediately for Poti in the Soviet Socialist Republic of Georgia, nowadays simply called the Republic of Georgia. In Poti, we would discharge the greatest portion of our cargo and remain there for at least six weeks.

In Odessa, we were discharging grain into barges alongside and we noted that these barges, as well as barges alongside other American ships in port, were moving across the harbor and being backloaded into Russian flag ships. We learned that these were bound for Iron Curtain, African, and Central American countries that were dependent upon the USSR to keep their own people fed.

In Poti, this was not the case. Our cargo was loaded dockside into open rail cars, when they were available, and it was our understanding this grain was bound for the interior of the Soviet Union. Due to the extended stay there, I had the most time to interact and learn about the people who inhabited this ancient country of the Caucasus Mountains and that had produced one of the most famous of the world's murderous tyrants of our lifetime, Josef Stalin.

"Stalin" was of course a nom de guerre, given to the man while in prison during the Russian Revolution. His real name was Jugashevili and that form of last name is itself testimony to his Georgian origin.

When going ashore in Poti, we were required to surrender our Merchant Mariners Document (alternately called seaman's papers or z-card) to the Soviet Army soldier who was stationed 24 hours per day at the foot of the gangway, monitoring all crew movements on and off the ship. We were in turn handed a green card that served as our identity card and shore pass. As it was covered in writing in the Cyrillic alphabet, we had no clue what it said.

This soldier could, if he chose to do so, thoroughly inspect our persons to ensure we were not taking any contraband with us. A small level of discretion in our behavior with this soldier would usually enable us to take black-market items ashore without being subject to a body search. But, if found to have something like a camera, for example, it would not only be confiscated but the person who had the camera, now suspected of espionage, would likely be restricted to the ship for the remainder of our stay and may even enjoy the experience of KGB interrogation.

One evening I went ashore with a pair of new Levi's jeans wrapped around my torso under my shirt and jacket and secured with duct tape. The exchange had been arranged by the first engineer and we rendezvoused with several Georgians in the alley between a couple of the usual large and ugly Soviet-style apartment buildings to remove the jeans and exchange them for a large bag of rubles.

When done, our new friends invited us for a drink at a nearby restaurant, just across the footbridge on the main street that crosses the canal through which the city's human waste flows to the Black Sea. It was the usual dull white tile restaurant, and we sat at a round table while the black marketers commenced ordering vodka, to be drunk in the typical Russian style.

This involved the waiter delivering a tray full of half-liter bottles of vodka, along with tall shot glasses (twice the size of an American shot glass) for each of the five of us, and the inevitable plate containing squares of semi-sweet chocolate that is placed in the center of the table and of which drinkers periodically take a piece to balance the taste of straight vodka in one's mouth.

Before long, the table was covered with partially empty half-liter vodka bottles and the floor around our table was littered with many bottles that were quite empty. Our three friends overcame the limits of their English and our Russian fluency with simple, clear demands that we "Drink! Drink!" They had a lifetime of daily consumption of vodka to bolster their endurance. I did not but, ever hard-headed, I bravely drank on with more gusto than sense.

At one point, not yet fully understanding the historical dynamic of Russia vs Georgia, I said something that more or less indicated that I was referring to our new friends as Russians. This was not taken well. One of our companions began to shout in a very loud voice something to the effect of: "ME NO RUSSKY, ME GEORGIAN!!" then made a pantomime gesture of holding a rifle to his shoulder and firing it, repeatedly saying: "ME KILL RUSSKY!!"

His partners chimed in with similar and equally loud agreement. This drew the rapt attention of everyone else in the place, including the two unmistakable government minders (presumed to be KGB) who had followed us into the restaurant. It did not seem to me that this public display of hatred for ethnic Russians could be good for us, nor indeed for our Georgian companions either, and we made haste to indicate we were overdue to return to the ship.

Unfortunately, the amount of straight vodka that I had consumed interfered mightily with my ability to walk and I was later informed that the first engineer, a large, robust, native of the state of Maine, found it necessary to carry me over his shoulder most of the way back to the dock. To this day, there are the deep indentations of my bicuspids in the lamination of my z-card, as it was necessary for me to clamp it in my teeth when it was returned to me by the soldier on the dock in order to free up both my hands to drag myself up the gangway and to my fo'c'sle.

Ships such as Maritime Longevity were used to transport grain to the USSR as détente took place. Author Leahy was in Black Sea ports for many weeks.

We were in Poti for May Day, the international Communist holiday. A group from our ship were invited by the Inflot Agent to attend the parade in the town square. Everyone went but, the radio operator made the perhaps understandable error of trying to take his camera with him. He and his camera were immediately sent back up the gangway never to go ashore in Poti again, but at least he did not lose his expensive camera and did not experience Soviet interrogation practices either. It could have been worse.

Due to the small size of the town, the parade consisted of the marching band from the port's Naval base assembled next to the reviewing stand and playing the Internationale ("Arise you victims of oppression, for the tyrants fear your might...") continuously, as groups from every business and industry in Poti marched proudly past. "Here come the Bakery Workers!!" We were assigned places of honor in the reviewing stands and for the humble representatives of the largest capitalist society in the world, it was an extraordinary day.

The next week was the 30th anniversary of the surrender of Berlin, the end of "The Great Patriotic War" as Russians and all Soviets called World War II. A ceremony was scheduled at the Seaman's Club that night with crew members of all the ships in port invited. The director of the Seaman's Club, after a lengthy and deeply moving presentation of the terrible suffering, privation, and death toll endured by the Soviet people before the final defeat of the Fascist enemy, requested that a representative of each crew from an Allied country say a few words on the subject of the war.

There were tables of Norwegians, French, British, and Canadians, in addition to our group of Americans. Each took turn briefly describing their part in the war as most everyone there was of an age to have participated in it. Some in their Navies, others on merchant ships.

When our turn came, although several of my shipmates were veterans of the war, we were a little uncomfortable. Being Americans, we were after all representing the other side of the great gulf that then existed between the two world "Superpowers". I found myself drafted to do the public speaking for the American contingent. I said that while I had been born shortly after the war, my father and one uncle had served in the U.S Navy during the war and my other uncle had been on American merchant ships on the Murmansk and Archangel runs. And I said it was to be hoped that the solidarity then enjoyed by all the Allied countries represented here tonight could continue for the future, as well.

When I mentioned that my uncle had been on the Murmansk and Archangel runs, all the Russians and other Soviets broke into furious applause, followed by the crews of other ships, particularly the Norwegians, who shouted that they too had been in those Allied convoys, and I knew then I had done the right thing by agreeing to say something on this occasion.

An opportunity for legitimate romance came my way while in Poti. There was a good seaman's club there, equipped with an actual sit-down bar and they even had canned orange juice from communist Algeria, making it possible to avoid drinking vodka either straight or with the only other mixer on offer: fruit nectar as thick as molasses.

One could combine Stolichnaya, the excellent Russian vodka used for export, with decent Algerian orange juice and have a perfectly acceptable screwdriver. There was also ample opportunity to speak at length in English with European seamen long accustomed to Americans' inability to speak other languages. Also, there were staff members and functionaries of the club that themselves spoke English with various degrees of fluency, and were anxious to practice and improve their language skills.

One such person was a lovely young lady named Luda (Ludmilla). She was in her early twenties and was from Kemerovo, in what was then Soviet Central Asia and is now known as Kazakhstan. She was in training to become an English-Russian translator with a professional goal of one day becoming a simultaneous translator at the United Nations. She had been sent by her teachers at the university in Kemerovo to attend at the Seaman's Club in Poti and work on development of her English skills.

Fortunately for me, I spoke fairly good English. Luda was a very beautiful girl and, when one says that a girl in the Soviet Union of that time is attractive, it should be understood as something beyond a beautiful girl as we know it while walking down a Manhattan street. As mentioned previously, Soviet women had no access to cosmetics or even simple toiletries. Even bars of Lux or Palmolive soap were deeply appreciated when given to a woman, or even a man for that matter.

Their dress was invariably threadbare, ill-fitting, and of the drabbest sort of print as ever found in a St. Vincent DePaul clothing bin. Only a lucky few had two dresses, so that one could be worn while the other washed. Most stayed at home until their one dress, having been washed, had time to dry. One does not realize how much help a Western woman gets with her appearance from all those nice products and clothes available to them. It is therefore a hard but accurate rule of life that, if a Russian woman appears especially attractive, it is the result of a gift from God, not Max Factor.

Luda and I grew close. To be honest, I was the only one around close to her young age and that probably gave me an edge in winning her interest. We were never able to consummate our relationship however, due to the unique and bizarre nature of Soviet determination to control the lives of everyone. We could not go to her home to be alone together because she had been sent to live in a one-bedroom apartment shared by three families and using a community bathroom and kitchen with the families of all other apartments on that floor.

This was a normal living situation in that place and time— multiple families sharing State-assigned apartments. Indeed, the head stevedore that was in charge of our ship's discharge operations boasted with evident pride that his recent promotion to that managerial position came with assignment to a private apartment for his wife and three children. Even though it was only one room, this was still a great perk in Soviet society.

I also could not simply take Luda to a hotel. To have done that would result in the Soviet Army soldier stationed in the lobby asking to see our papers before I could register for a room. On inspection of my shore pass he would have told me I had no need of a hotel room and should go back to my ship and tell Luda to go home to the apartment the State had generously assigned to her.

I need hardly say at this point that I could never have gotten Luda onboard my ship, either. In desperation one night, we decided to try to achieve a little horizontal mambo in the darkness of a local park but, once again, a patrolling soldier did his duty and prevented that. After I sailed away to return to America, Luda and I remained in correspondence, sending letters to each other for a year or so. In those Cold War days, when a letter from Luda arrived in my mailbox in Texas, coming as it was from the Soviet Union, it was obvious that it had been opened and carelessly resealed multiple times by government censors on both ends, but I think just a few years earlier we would have not been able to write to each other at all. I sometimes wonder if Luda ever realized her dream to come to New York as a U.N. translator.

Our return voyage to the U.S. began with a notable day while transiting the Aegean Sea after clearing the Dardanelles. Our chief steward had acquired a live goat from the market and the cook butchered it and set up a grill that the engineers fabricated from and old oil drum on the ship's fantail.

While the goat grilled, those of us not on watch gathered on the fantail, drinking a pretty decent Russian brandy that the steward had got his hands on, and smoking the Cuban cigars that were non-existent in America since the 1959 embargo started. We looked out on the deep blue of the Aegean Sea and the Greek Islands with their whitewashed buildings gleaming in the sun that we were passing. We reflected that while many people had to pay a great deal of money to make a voyage like this, through some of the most beautiful waters in the world, we were here enjoying it all and being paid to do so. While it is true that we were on a rusty old tanker, not a pretty passenger ship well ... a small trade-off for the greater benefit.

The trip back to the U.S. was, well, eventful. But, like the full tale of how our ship came to run aground directly across the ship channel of the Bolivar Roads at the beginning of that voyage, those stories must wait for telling at another time.

Desert Shield and Desert Storm
Leahy

In the Fall of 1990, President Bush decided that the invasion of Kuwait by Iraqi forces would require military intervention to halt it before it carried on to Saudi Arabia. The Navy branch called the Military Sealift Command (MSC) immediately advised the U.S. Maritime Administration (MarAd) that they would need to activate the former commercial ships held in deactivated state in the three National Defense Reserve Fleets (NDRF).

These ships were primarily break bulk freighters and some tankers, and were nearly all steam-propulsion vessels. The USCG announced that the officers and crewmembers of the U.S. Merchant Marine would now be under their direction in accordance with the oath of allegiance we all take when first receiving our seaman's papers. On that basis, the American seamen's unions advised us that all officers and crew currently onboard operating ships would remain there, and no reliefs would be available for the foreseeable future.

Those of us ashore on vacation or otherwise were soon being assigned to the ships being activated out of the NDRF fleets. Eventually, we activated eighty (80) mothballed ships, tested them, manned them with crews, and began loading munitions and other supplies to support Operation Desert Shield and, when the conflict actually began in January of 1991, Operation Desert Storm.

Due to the years of constant reduction in the size of the American Merchant Marine, the pool of available, qualified American mariners was soon beginning to run dry. Officers who had retired after a long career at sea or had quit going to sea and taken up unrelated careers found themselves getting phone calls from the USCG. In the case of these former ships' officers who had left the industry and whose licenses had expired, the USCG waived the re-examination requirement, issued them new licenses, and sent them out to whatever ship they were qualified to serve in.

Any former enlistee in the Navy, preferably with an honorable discharge but not necessarily, could go down to the nearest USCG Marine Inspection Office and soon find himself with a Z-Card (seaman's papers). By the time we had all eighty of these reserve fleet ships crewed up there was not a seaman left in America and quite a few people of all ages who had never been onboard a ship in their life now found themselves members, at least for the time being, of the U.S. Merchant Marine and one of the various maritime unions, as well.

I was ashore on vacation when the call went out and was soon was assigned to a group of steam engineers who specialize in starting up the steam plants of ships that had been long shut down, cold and inactive. The group I was with in the Port Arthur, Texas, area started up eleven ships, directed repairs by local shipyards, tested and trialed them for the USCG and American Bureau of Shipping Inspectors. We then turned them over to the crews who were taking them to the Naval ammunition depots on the East and West Coasts for loading and departure for the Persian Gulf. After that, I was assigned as 1st engineer to a ship loading ammo in North Carolina that was proving to be especially difficult to get into a condition of reliable seaworthiness.

The chief engineer and I had sailed together before and he had requested me due to the lack of experience of all his officers and crew except the second engineer and electrician. The captain had been called back from a well-deserved retirement from the sea, and the chief mate had left his seagoing career years before to become a Wall Street stockbroker.

Fortunately, both these men had sailed on old, retired, freighters just like this one and therefore understood the cargo gear and how to load them, so that turned out to be a blessing. In the engine room, we were still repairing machinery and testing it for USCG inspectors while the cargo-loading of munitions continued out on deck and in the holds.

U.S. Merchant Marine rushed all types of equipment to Saudi Arabia on ships activated from the National Defense Reserve Force.

I soon learned that not only was America running short of mariners who were experienced in operating these steam-powered break bulk freighters, but we were also short of longshoremen and stevedores who had experience in the very specialized skills of loading munitions into these types of ships.

The longshoremen were also expected to operate the cargo gear onboard ship, to lift the ammunition from dock into the cargo hold by the old "yard and stay" method. Many current dockworkers had never done this either. Such cargo loading in these ships had not been done since the end of the Vietnam War and therefore retired longshoremen and stevedores had to be called back into service to guide their contemporary brothers in the proper methods of safely stowing this cargo.

Not for the first time or last time in the Desert Shield/Desert Storm sealift did I see retired ships, retired seamen, and retired longshoremen called upon to dust off their old skills to support America at war.

A couple of weeks later, all cargo was loaded and the longshoremen and deck gang were closing up the holds and securing for sea when I got a call down below that a Navy rep was headed my way and I should escort him throughout the machinery spaces. It turned out that a discrepancy of one whole pallet of 9-millimeter ammunition had been found in the cargo manifest.

I escorted the Navy man through every cubic inch of the machinery spaces starting in the engine room, down through the engine room bilges, through the shaft alley to the stern, up through the steering gear room, all over the boilers up to the top of the stack. No contraband or anything else was found. I did ask how he thought a crew member could clandestinely transport a pallet of ammo from the main deck to these remote spaces, but he assured me logical thought was of no significance in this case. It was finally decided that the clerks and checkers must have made an error in their paperwork.

Early the next morning, I was standing at the main engine throttles with the 8-12 3rd engineer and his oiler nearby. The 2nd engineer, together with two of his firemen, was positioned in front of the boilers. Our ship was outbound on the Cape Fear River, bound initially for Gibraltar for bunkers, with a final destination that was classified and thereby unknown to us.

The Cape Fear River is not a particularly wide waterway and considering it leads to the only ammunition depot on the East Coast, it was at that time a very heavily trafficked channel. It was not too long before I got a red light and audio alarm telling me the port steering gear had just failed. Pretty much simultaneously the sound-powered phone from the bridge rang, with a deeply distressed captain shouting they had no steering and an inbound ship was fast approaching up the river.

The bridge crew was powerless to steer a ship, fully laden with munitions, down the river with another ship coming toward them. I could hear a lot of shouting through the phone, even over the engine room noise that filtered through the phone booth acoustic panels. What needed to be done was crystal clear, but not easily accomplished. I had to go back to the steering gear room at the ship's stern to change over to the starboard unit, but I also was required to be standing by right where I was, handling the engine throttles. Either the 1st engineer or the chief must standby the throttles in maneuvering waters like this river, just as the captain must be in person on the navigating bridge.

I quickly changed the switch on the sound powered phone to the chief's office and called to tell him I had to go change over the steering gear and to please come immediately down below to cover me on the throttles. I started climbing the four levels of inclined ladders to the main deck, then outside and down the deck, vaulting over the heavy chains that secured the tanker trucks on top of the cargo hatches. Then I went through the watertight door and down the ladder to the steering gear flat, killed power to the failed port steering unit, energized power to the starboard system, and manually changed over the six-way valve that directs hydraulic fluid from either one system or the other to the rams.

Very soon I saw the rudder post yokes begin to move and the steering gear was again answering the wheel on the bridge. A quick call to the captain on the bridge confirmed that they had regained control of the ship and were now passing the inbound ship safely. A second call to the engine room confirmed the chief was there on the throttles.

I went up on deck and decided to take a quick smoke break as I waved to the passing inbound ship and reflected for a moment on how close we had all just come to the end of our lives. It was a bracing start for this voyage to Desert Storm.

We headed across the Atlantic for the Mediterranean Sea. From Gibraltar onward, I do not think we were ever without another gray-hulled American ship within our sight. At choke points like Gib and Suez there were many to be seen. The U.S.

fleets of sealift support ships, all with civilian crews, were by this point both headed toward the Persian Gulf and returning from there to the U.S. to load another cargo.

We arrived at Port Said one afternoon, dropped anchor and took steam off the main engine to await our turn to transit the Suez Canal. When I came up on deck from the engine room that afternoon I walked into a familiar, but in this case unexpected, sight.

Ships at anchor at Port Said awaiting transit are quickly boarded by dozens of local vendors who set up shops all over the main deck selling souvenirs. Often these are beautifully hammered silver, brass, and copper works of art, but some are just junk. Photo Sami is a reliable presence, having taken photos of the ship at anchor from his launch, he enlarges them, mounts them in hand-carved wooden frames painted in shiny gold, and sells them to interested crew members.

Scrap dealers come aboard looking for the mate and bo'sn to purchase old, worn out mooring lines and also seeking the 1st engineer to purchase the scrap brass fittings that are always accumulated from piping repairs and saved for this purpose.

There is usually at least one barber and there are also a few thieves against whom the experienced crew ensures all doors to the interior of the ship are locked and for whom they remain alert.

On this occasion, however, I was surprised to emerge from the accommodation house into the sights, sounds, and smells of a large Arab souq, with trading activities in full swing all over the ship's deck. Dozens of these U.S. ships carrying munitions were transiting the Suez Canal at this time, several each day. What a place for a well-planned act of sabotage to cripple our effort to support the military build-up in Saudi Arabia and to interfere with world seaborne commerce for an extended period as well.

I looked around at all the local folks on the deck and asked myself who could know if all these people in customary Arab dress were Egyptians, or could a few of them be Iraqi saboteurs? Well, no ammunitions ships were blown up in the Suez Canal during Desert Shield, Storm, or Saber so, either the intelligence forces of Egypt and the U.S. had the matter well under control behind the scenes or else Saddam Hussein's folks were too busy to think of it.

A container ship appearing to be on the sand while transiting the Suez Canal. The canal is 250 feet wide, running 120 miles through the desert, without any locks. Photo courtesy of Leahy.

I began a tour around the deck (or through the bazaar if you like) in search of a barber. Passing around the fantail at the stern, I saw one enterprising fellow had brought a charcoal brazier aboard, set it up back there where it would hopefully go unnoticed by anyone in authority, and was grilling lamb kebobs. They were excellent and a nice change from generally spice-free shipboard cuisine. I found the barber had set up his shop at a set of large mooring line bitts which served as his barber chair, and sat down.

He thoughtfully threw a large cloth over my sweat-soaked and black oil-stained white boiler suit, so no loose hairs would get on it. I removed the equally sweat-soaked bandana from by head and he poured a pot of water over it to rinse out at least some of the sweat salt, then set to work trimming my hair. He finished off with a remarkably close straight razor shave and praised me for my good sense in keeping my moustache. A $10 bill of U.S. currency was such a satisfactory payment for him that he gave me a nice barber's set of straight razor, scissors, and comb. I still have the scissors and razor.

We heaved anchor and began transit of the Canal at first light the next morning. I went below at 0430 to put steam on the engine and generally ready the engine room and crew for the day's work ahead. We would not be having any machinery failures while transiting the Canal if I could prevent it; this was not the place to have something go wrong.

At noon, the chief came down to relieve me on the throttles for lunch and I went out on deck for a smoke. On either side of the Canal in this area were desert sand dunes, mostly uninterrupted by vegetation. Several old rusting Egyptian tanks were to be seen, as well as the occasional concrete building pock marked with shell holes and other artillery damage. These were remnants of the Six Day War, when Israel was simultaneously attacked by its Arab neighbors on all sides, and required just six days to achieve the surrender of their opponents.

After dropping the Canal pilot at Suez City, we sailed down the Red Sea, passing Mecca, Medina, Eritrea, and through the tight squeeze at Djibouti and Yemen. We turned the corner in to the Gulf of Aden and followed more or less parallel to the coasts of Yemen and Oman into the Arabian Sea and onward toward the Straits of Hormuz.

That hot desert wind was the only source of air for the ventilator fans to blow into the even hotter engine room and it was like Hell down there. Whenever we stood still a pool of sweat developed on the floor plates around us and we were eating salt tablets like candy. This is the reason I had avoided sailing on ships to the Persian Gulf during my seagoing career, but Desert Storm took that option out of my hands.

At breakfast in the officers' saloon one morning I learned we were approaching the Straits of Hormuz and would shortly be in that tightly controlled choke point. The captain was herding our two apprentice radio operators away from the breakfast table and up to their radio shack to standby for orders from the Navy in this critical AOR.

Since we had two completely inexperienced apprentices in lieu of one fully qualified radio officer, these two gentlemen were the bane of the captain's life. He both addressed them and referred to them as "Frick and Frack" or, alternately, the "Gold Dust Twins" and never referred to either of them individually.

The Straits are not pilot waters, and although transiting them does not require us to be on standby for ship maneuvering orders, I decided it would be prudent of me to drop down below and be on standby with the 3rd engineer on watch. I also had the 2nd go down and standby the boilers with an extra fireman, as well.

Soon I heard the horn indicating a call on the sound-powered telephone and the 3rd was waving at me to take the call. It was the third mate on watch on the bridge. He was an old friend and shipmate from tanker days and a solid, reliable, deck officer. He told me he was really glad I was down below due to the Straits being congested with many warships and they all seemed to be maintaining radio silence. Actually, we were supposed to know that already, but Frick and Frack had not bothered to pass that message on to the officer of the watch or the captain, either. Apparently, they did not consider this urgent information.

The chief engineer and I made sure one of us was standing by the throttles during the transit of the Straits. That afternoon proved this to have been a good idea. The Old Man called down to warn me he might need to change speeds and also directed me to start up the main fire pump and pressurize the deck fire stations to repel boarders.

We were in the tightest point of the Straits and Iranian pirates were pursuing us from astern with three speedboats while another speedboat was ahead of us and forcing the ship to change course repeatedly to avoid the boat.

This is common technique where the attention of the bridge team is focused on the boat crossing back and forth across the bow while the other boats come up under the stern frame and try to board using grappling hooks and line. This pirate "attack" had nothing whatsoever to do with Desert Storm, Iraq, Kuwait, the

U.S., or the daily geopolitical crises of the Middle East. The Persians/Iranians living in this area had been boarding passing ships and stealing what they could for centuries. The fact that these many ships passing through their waters were loaded with munitions and other military cargo did not matter to them in the least. In point of fact, they were probably unaware of what was going on with all these gray-hulled ships and aircraft in the sky and cared not at all. A ship passes and they try to board it and steal what they can, just like their forefathers had done for time immemorial.

When we reached Ad Dammam, we dropped anchor along with numerous other American gray hulls already there and awaited our turn to shift to the dock. The dock area where we unloaded was a vast laydown area, perhaps the size of a dozen football fields. It was covered with tanks, helicopters, Humvees, tanker trucks etc. We had mobilized more equipment to support this war than was even required to be put into use on the battlefields.

Postscript:

When we returned to the U.S. from this trip, loaded with returning military equipment, our discharge port was Savannah, Georgia. While we were maneuvering up the river, the chief engineer came down below and told me he would cover the throttles so I could go up above and just have a look at what was happening up there.

I emerged on deck just as the ship took a bend in the river and a public square downtown was revealed, right on the riverside. There was a brass band playing Souza marches and the square was packed with local citizens waving and yelling. There were American flags and red, white, and blue bunting. Welcoming us home. Looking over the side, I realized our ship was surrounded with private boats and those people too were yelling "Welcome Home," "Congratulations," and even "Thank You." The good citizens in those boats were throwing cans of cold beer up to those of us on the deck. All the crew that was not required on watch had come out to see this. What a different experience from the last time ships like these had returned home from the Vietnam War. Thank you, Savannah. We will never forget.

SS Santa Ana, a freighter on drydock, Mobile, AL, after return from Desert Storm. Author's son, Daniel Leahy, stands under the propeller. Daniel is now a marine diesel engineer in a Mobile shipyard. Photo by Leahy.

Arriving back in port, a scene repeated through the ages of sea travel. Here a tanker sails toward the Golden Gate Bridge and San Francisco, CA, as the sun rises off the bow. Photo by Leahy.

Additional Materials

Here we provide terms and explanations useful to fully understand the details of *Sea Stories*. First are additional resources, including books about Galveston. Second is a glossary of maritime terms—if you want to know what a plimsoll mark is, it is here. Ships come in all shapes, built around their functions, as described in the third section. How mariners operate the ships is found in the chain of command. Hint: The captain and the chief engineer both report to the same person ashore.

Good news, none of this will be on the exam.

For further information on Galveston:

Kimber Fountain's Galveston Books online at Amazon:
The Maceos and The Free State of Galveston: An Authorized History, *2018*

Galveston's Red Light District: A History of The Line, *2019*

Galveston Seawall Chronicles, *2017*
For tours of Galveston see:
www.facebook.com/AuthorKimberFountain

To learn more about Galveston & its connection to the sea:

Bill Cherry's Galveston Memories, by William Cherry
VanJus Press, Galveston, Texas, 2000

Galveston: A History, by David G. McComb
University of Texas-Austin Press, 1986

Galveston Wharf Stories: Characters, Captains & Cruises
by Alvin L. Sallee, www.amazon.com 2019

Handbook of Texas Online, Edward Coyle Sealy
Galveston Wharves
www.tshaonline.org

Ray Miller's Galveston, by Ray Miller
Capital Printing, Austin, Texas, 1983

Recalled Recollections by I. H. Kempner
The Egan Company, Dallas Texas, 1981

Women, Culture and Community by Elizabeth Hayes Turner,
Oxford Press, New York, 1997

Galveston: A History of the Island by Gary Cartwright
Atheneum, New York, 1991

The Storm of the Century by Al Roker
Harper Collins, New York, 2015

Caribbean, by James A. Michener
Random House, NY, 1989

Glossary of Maritime Terminology

The following is a list of terms and expressions found in the stories of seagoing life that may be unfamiliar to those who are not themselves mariners. Compiled by authors.

ARRIVAL/DEPARTURE: A ship's official arrival time and departure time is established at the bar, not a berth. (Example: "the SS *Ocean Queen* took Arrival at 0235 on 14 May 2011 and subsequently took Departure at 1756 on 17 May 2011".)

BACK AFT: Opposite of Up Forward.

BAR: The bar is the entry point of any port. It refers to the sandbar commonly found at the entrance to ship channels and dredged to accommodate the draft of ships entering and leaving the port

BERTH: When used as a verb, this means the act of bringing a ship into a wharf or pier. (Example: "The ship will be berthing at

Pier 41 this evening.") When used as a noun, it is a generic term for a pier, wharf, or dock. It can also be used as a noun to refer to a job on a ship. (Example: "I caught a berth on a tanker bound for Venezuela").

BOLLARD: A strong post on the wharf where a ship's lines (ropes) are looped over to keep the vessel moored to the pier.

BRIDGE: The deck where the navigation area of the ship is located. The actual navigation space is called the wheelhouse but wheelhouse and bridge can be used interchangeably.

BULK CARRIER: This type of ships is designed to carry dry cargos in loose, bulk form, i.e. grain.

BULKHEAD: Ship's name for a "wall".

CHIEF: Only the ship's chief engineer is referred to and addressed as Chief.

CONTAINER SHIP: They carry exclusively containers in which all the various items of break bulk cargo have already been stowed. Most containers are 40 feet long although smaller ones are 20 feet long and this is the basis for establishing the cargo carrying capacity of such a ship as a specific number of "TEU's", which stand for "twenty foot equivalent units".

CREW: The word can have two meanings, depending on the context in which it is used. It can refer only to the unlicensed crew members to differentiate them from the officers or it can refer to the entire complement of the ship, both officers and unlicensed.

CRIMPS & BOARDING MASTERS: Criminals who haunted the waterfronts, being paid by ship owners or shipmasters to Shanghai seamen to fill out crews. The Merchant Marine Act of 1915 made these actions illegal.

DECK: Ship's name for a "floor".

DEEP SEA SHIP: Refers to large ships engaged in trade on the open oceans, as opposed to near coastal waters or rivers and bays.

DOWN BELOW: Opposite of Up Above.

EOT: The engine order telegraph is a piece of wheelhouse equipment that is used to give engine orders to the engineers below from the bridge when the ship is maneuvering.

EQUATOR CLUB: It is traditional when a new seaman on a ship at sea crosses the Equator for the first time to subject him to some form of hazing, to welcome him into the "Equator Club".

ETA/ETB: Estimated Time of Arrival (at the Bar) and Estimated Time of Berthing (at the Dock). A ship may be delayed at anchorage for some period of time before proceeding to a berth.

FLOP: An old expression for a temporary living arrangement while ashore. A flop might be a cheap hotel room, a girlfriend's apartment, a room rented by the week above a seafarer's bar or even a cathouse. It is a shortened version of the old expression: flophouse.

FORECASTLE: (abbreviated as "fo'c'sle and pronounced as FOLK-sul). The word is a very old nautical term and can have several meanings depending on the context in which it is used. The fo'c'sle is the forwardmost part of the ship's hull which on traditional ship designs resembles a castle. It can also be used to refer to the sleeping quarters of unlicensed crewmembers, regardless of their specific location onboard the ship.

FOREIGN ARTICLES: A written contract signed by the master and each crew member, committing the crewmembers to a set period of time, usually six-months or twelve months, that they will remain onboard the ship in their position unless released by the master by "mutual consent".

GANGWAY: The device deployed between a ship's deck and adjacent wharf to enable persons to cross between the dock and the vessel.

GOLD FIX: Getting a draw of cash from the captain against a crewmember's accumulated earned wages.

HEAD: Name for bathroom on a ship.

IRON MIKE: Term used for what would be considered an "autopilot" on an aircraft. Automatic steering machinery that can be connected to the steering system. "Put it on hand" is the verbal command used to direct the helmsman to switch off the Iron Mike and take over hand control of the steering himself.

LOG BOOKS: Two official log books are maintained on a ship, one on the bridge and one in the engine room. Every significant detail is scrupulously entered. Falsification of any of these books is a criminal act.

LONGSHOREMAN: The skilled dockside workers who load, unload and otherwise handle cargo to and from a ship.

OLD MAN: A nickname for the captain of any ship. It is not derogatory. It is used in reference to the captain but not used to address him directly.

ON THE BEACH: A seaman's expression for being ashore and not having a berth on a ship but seeking one.

ON THE HOOK: A ship at anchor is said to be on the hook.

PILOT: A captain who has expert local knowledge of the channel between the bar and berth in any particular port. On the bridge, they are referred to as pilot. The captain (master) of a vessel does not surrender his ultimate responsibility to a pilot, except at the Panama and Suez Canals.

PIERHEAD JUMP: All officers and crew are required to be back aboard a ship no less than one hour prior to her scheduled sailing time. If a new crew member is assigned (shipped) to the vessel at the last minute and must join the ship just before she begins to cast off mooring lines, they are said to have a pierhead jump. It is a reference to literally jumping from the pier to the pilot ladder after the gangway or accommodation ladder has be secured for sea although that risky act rarely occurs at the gangway is held deployed until the crew members gets aboard.

PILOT WATERS: The waters thru which a ship passes when transiting between the bar and a berth where a local pilot is required to be aboard.

PLANK OWNER: A member of the crew of a U.S. Navy ship or Coast Guard cutter when that ship was originally commissioned.

PLIMSOLL MARK: Is a circle with a horizontal line through it and other markings. The marks are determined by the load on the ship and the draft of the ship so it is not top heavy or sitting too deep in the water. Marks welded and painted on both sides of the ship as specified by the vessel's class society to identify the maximum allowable draft when loaded to ensure safe stability. It allows for the density differences of salt, fresh and tropical waters.

RACK: Name for a bed on a ship. It can also be called a bunk or a padded shelf.

RO-RO SHIPS: These large ships are designed to carry all types of vehicles, aka "rolling stock".

SAILING BOARD: A large chalk board posted on deck near the gangway to advise crew members going ashore or returning of the date and time the ship is scheduled to sail (leave the dock).

SCHOONER-RIGGED: A crew member joining a ship without any personal gear whatsoever, just the clothes on his back. This can often occur in conjunction with the aforementioned "pierhead jump".

SEALIFT: A term used by the Navy and Merchant Marine to refer to operations of transporting military operation support materials, supplies and equipment.

SHANGHAI: this term refers to the practice of forcibly kidnaping seamen (or even unlucky non-seamen in the wrong place and time) and pressing them into service against their will. It was outlawed by the US Merchant Marine Act of 1915.

SHIPPING BOARD: A usually full wall-size board in a seamen's union hall where various jobs on various ships and their intended destination are listed so that union members can decide if they want to throw in on a particular job. If more than one member throws in his shipping card on the same job, a very specific set of shipping rules based on seniority are employed to decide who gets the job.

SLOP CHEST: The duty-free store onboard a ship sailing outside the US that carries cigarettes, beverages, underwear, work clothing, toiletries and similar goods to which seamen would otherwise have no access while at sea.

STEVEDORES: Stevedoring companies are contracted by cargo owners to load and unload the cargo from a ship. The Stevedores in turn hire and supervise the longshoremen.

SUITCASE BRIGADE: A large number of crewmembers deciding to get off a ship and give up their job after a periodic payoff and prior to signing a new set of foreign articles.

TANKER: A ship specifically designed to carry liquid cargo in bulk. These ships have very little cargo gear showing on deck as the large pumps for discharging cargo are below decks.

TURN TO: The act of reporting for work at one's duty station. (Example: "He turned to for his watch at 1150").

USCG: United States Coast Guard. All U.S. flag ships and their crews are inspected and certified by the USCG.

UP ABOVE: Directional expression indicating a place higher up vertically in the ship than where the speaker is located.

UP FORWARD: Directional expression indicating a place in the direction of the ship's bow from where the speaker is located.

WHARF: A generic term for dock, pier, or berth. Different locations and ports may use any of these terms to identify the same thing.

Ships Come in All Shapes
Sallee

Ships of all kinds transit the Panama Canal.

Ships on the high seas come in various types depending chiefly on the cargo they carry. **Container ships** carry rectangle steel boxes perfect for toys, furniture, running shoes or any packaged item. The containers come in 20-foot-equivalent units (TEU's) or 40-foot lengths, and can be loaded like building blocks above and below decks. Huge dockside gantry cranes, up to 150 feet tall with cabs high above, reach cables down and quickly grasp the four corners of each container and whisk it up, over, and down onto a train or truck below.

A container ship in Cartagena, Columbia, with stacks of 20-foot unit, or TEU, containers.

Break bulk cargo ships are designed for carrying all sorts of cargo which has not been consolidated into containers. These ships have complex cargo-handling gear on their main decks including kingposts, crosstrees, booms, and winches to operate the wire ropes on all of the above. In Galveston, windmill blades over half a football field long, boats, manufacturing materials and even ship propellers can be seen being loaded or unloaded from break bulk ships.

In the past, break bulk carriers even had cabins for passengers. Today, any cargo ship company willing to take passengers usually only takes 12, as regulations require a doctor on board for 13 or more passengers. You must also be under 70 years old and in excellent health. Most trips are 30 to 45 days in length. Alvin tried for the last few years of his 60s to hop aboard a working cargo ship, without luck. He did make some new friends in the process, nonetheless.

Bulk carriers handle loose items, such as grain. For example, the first story in chapter two tells the story of the crew of the Drogba, which was loaded in Galveston with one-inch ball-bearing-size soy balls and lots of dust.

A bulk carrier, Spar Taurus, about to load grain at Pier 39 in Galveston Harbor.

Tankers with complex piping systems carry various liquid cargoes in bulk. They range from single-grade crude oil ships to multi-grade petroleum product and chemical ships. Product tankers may carry anything from all grades of jet fuel, gasoline, diesel, aviation gas, even potable water. Some chemical and petroleum product tankers have cargo systems that enable them to carry as many as 40 different segregated grades of products. Seamen traditionally refer to these tankers as "drug stores."

A tanker transits Gatun Lake, part of the Panama Canal.

Sulphur tankers must heat the sulfur to keep it in a molten state for pumping in and out of the ship. Sulfur, which may be mined or can be a byproduct of crude oil processing, is used as a fertilizer, often in Africa.

The SS Marine Duval, originally built as a T-2 tanker during WWII, was such a tanker based at the sulfur terminal in Galveston from 1970 until being sent to the breakers yard in India in 2002.

Alvin's friend, Asher Spalding, who has sailed on similar ships, is not a fan. The heat and smell are not pleasant to say the least, and the cloud of sulfur vapor in which the ship is always enveloped causes rapid deterioration of everything on and in these ships.

Roll on, roll off ships—Ro/Ro's—are floating enclosed parking lots, hauling autos, tractors and trucks. Appearing as massive windowless buildings with a few small cubicles topside, these ships come with their own fold-down ramps off the stern. The Wallenius and Wilhelmsen line delivers up to three acres of BMW cars to Galveston some months.

The Parsifal, a roll on, roll off ship on Gatun Lake carrying cars on interior decks.

And least, but never last, **cruise ships**, those built as floating hotels, and those like SS United States, which was built for the open ocean. From the huge oasis class to those which are wind-aided, and hold only a few hundred guests. And those, as with Fritz Damler's sailboat, that in years past you could crew for $10 a day and ride the waves of up to 35 feet in a boat the same length.

A Carnival cruise ship tied up to Pier 21 behind the masts of the tall ship Elissa in Galveston Harbor.

Chain of Command on Merchant Ships
Leahy

Senior Officers:
CAPTAIN & CHIEF ENGINEER: The captain is the senior officer and head of the deck Department, and the chief engineer is senior officer and head of the engine department. They both report directly to the shoreside manager for the vessel, usually called the port engineer. In addition, in his capacity as ship's master, the captain has overarching responsibility for the cargo, crew, and

vessel itself when the ship is at sea. The equivalent naval rank is captain for both positions.

CHIEF MATE & FIRST ENGINEER: The chief mate is second senior officer of the deck department and the first engineer is second senior officer of the engine department. All members of their respective departments report to them, and they report directly to the captain and chief, respectively. The equivalent naval rank is commander for both positions.

Other Officers:

2ND and 3RD MATES/2ND and 3RD ENGINEERS: These officers are the officers of the watch (OOW) for the bridge and engine room, respectively. Crewmembers assigned to their watches report to them during their watches. The equivalent naval ranks are lieutenant commander for the 2nd and lieutenant for the 3rd, whether mate or engineer.

Unlicensed Crew:

The unlicensed crew members for the deck, engine, and steward departments consist of a "key rating" for each department (bo'sn for the deck, pumpman or electrician for the engine, and chief steward for the steward department). In addition, there are the watch standing crewmembers for deck and engine and various cooks and galley hands for the steward. Except for the entry rating for each department, all these crewmembers require accumulated sea time and written testing by the USCG to acquire the endorsements for their positions.

Note regarding the position of chief steward: On ocean-going, deep sea ships of the American Merchant Marine, the chief steward is a key rating and not an officer. However, on U.S. ships sailing on the Great Lakes only, the chief steward is considered an officer. He reports to the captain in either case.

The chain of command began on sailing ships many years ago. Here the SV Elissa out of Galveston is still sailed under a strict chain of command.

Made in the USA
Columbia, SC
29 May 2021

38377914R00128